Seven Heroes:

Medal of Honor Stories of the War in the Pacific

Sergeant Mitchell Paige, United States Marine Corps, won his Medal of Honor for bravery exhibited at Guadalcanal. Lieutenant Arthur Murray Preston, skipper of one of the torpedo boat squadrons in the Pacific, rescued a downed pilot in Wasile Bay in a mission that was called suicide from its onset.

Here are seven men of the Navy and the Marine Corps who showed "courage above and beyond the call of duty" and were rewarded with our nation's highest wartime citation.

The author brings to the reader the excitement and action of the events that led to each man's Medal, portraying the valor, and sometimes the tragedy, of the moment.

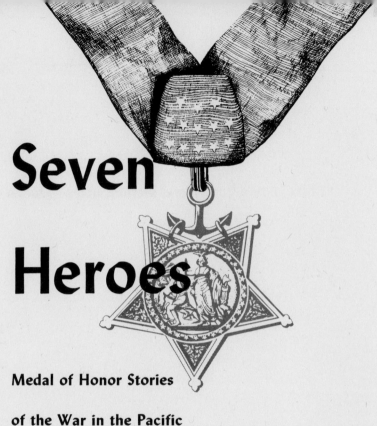

Seven

Heroes

Medal of Honor Stories

of the War in the Pacific

By Saul Braun

G. P. Putnam's Sons   New York

To my father and mother, and to Marcia

Published simultaneously in the Dominion of
Canada by Longmans Canada Limited, Toronto
Library of Congress Catalog Card Number:
65-20671
PRINTED IN THE UNITED STATES OF AMERICA
12216

Contents

Captain Henry Talmadge Elrod

1
THE FATTED CALVES

~~~~~~

CAPTAIN HENRY ELROD

Marine Fighter Squadron 211

DECEMBER 8-23, 1941

O<small>N THE</small> morning of November 28, 1941, twelve pilots of Marine Fighter Squadron (VMF) 211 flew their new F4F-3 Grumman Wildcats from the Ford Island Naval Air Station at Pearl Harbor onto the deck of the aircraft carrier *Enterprise.* The pilots had been told by their squadron leader, Major Paul Putnam, that they were going out for some experimental work, and would not be gone longer than two days, so they brought with them only the clothes they wore and small overnight kits.

At Ford Island, one of the planes had had trouble starting. Normally, its pilot would simply have washed out and remained at Pearl to idle away his free hours until the squadron returned. This time, however, the pilot was ferried to the carrier and, on arrival, issued one of *Enterprise's* own Wildcats. An unusual procedure, the pilots agreed. Several of the flyers made the logical deduction that Fighter Squadron 211 was not going on a practice cruise at all, but was making an indefinite or, perhaps, permanent change of station. Only Major Putnam had been told that VMF-211 was heading for Wake Island.

For many years a bird sanctuary, Wake Island had first been discovered in the sixteenth century by a Spaniard and was claimed in a desultory, offhand way by the United States in 1899, but was otherwise unwanted. Wake came under Navy jurisdiction in 1939, by which time much of Europe was at war and many thoughtful men agreed that time was also running out on the peaceful Pacific. "By the fall of 1940, we had known that war with Japan was inevitable," wrote Admiral William Halsey, "By the next spring, we knew it was impending." That spring, Admiral Husband Kimmel wrote a letter in which he suggested that "it appears not unlikely that one of the initial operations of the Japanese may be directed against Wake."

The bird sanctuary which for centuries only boatswain and frigate birds, terns and boobies had found tenable suddenly acquired vast strategic importance and was, along with Midway, Johnston and Palmyra, being thought of as a picket island, a sort of stationary aircraft carrier. In January, 1941, civilian contractors arrived to dredge a channel in the lagoon and to build roads, buildings, and a 30-foot-wide, 5,000-foot airstrip. A defense battalion of Marines, half strength, arrived in two sections during August and November and built installations for 5-inch shore guns. At a top secret conference in Pearl Harbor on November 27, it was decided that a squadron of Marine fighters should go to Wake im-

8

mediately. Putnam's squadron was selected and the following morning they were on their way.

Even if their suspicions had not otherwise been aroused, the Marine pilots would have known something was afoot by Admiral Halsey's Battle Order No. 1, promulgated as soon as the task force was at sea. "The *Enterprise* is now operating under war conditions," it stated. Scout pilots were instructed to sink all shipping and shoot all planes on sight.

Halsey's order was a shocker. What was he doing, some of the officers muttered, trying to start his own war? Halsey's intention was to see to it that 12 Wildcats in top condition landed at Wake without interference; nothing more.

Not only the fighter planes, but the pilots as well received the sort of care usually reserved for state treasures. The enthusiasm with which the ship's officers shared their quarters, their good food, and even their clothes with Putnam's pilots could hardly have been equaled. In a letter to Colonel Claude Larkin, commanding officer of Marine Air Group 21, written the day before arriving at Wake, Putnam noted, "I feel a bit like the fatted calf being groomed for whatever it is that happens to fatted calves." Putnam was to find out shortly.

On the morning of December 4, all hands who could went topside to wave off the Wildcats. Escorted by six dive bombers of the carrier's scouting squadron, and a PBY Catalina which had come out from Wake to lead them in, Putnam's pilots flew the last 175 miles to the submerged volcano—the top of which stuck up only 15 feet out of the sea—which was Wake Island.

The fighters circled the airfield once and in the proc-

9

ess got a good look at their new home. The atoll Wake actually consists of three islands named Peale, Wilkes and Wake, in the shape of a wishbone with the open ends pointing west, encircled by a coral reef. The largest island, Wake, is itself V-shaped; Peale extends the upper leg, Wilkes, the lower. All three are flat and covered with a random stubble of gnarled spiny brush which has for centuries been lashed by the Pacific winds.

The newly completed airfield had been cut into Wake Island at the southeast corner, where the two legs of the V met. The 12 Wildcats were the first fighter planes to appear at Wake (as it turned out, also the last) and so had been eagerly anticipated. The Marine flyers were met with what could fairly be called a tumultuous welcome. The island's entire population turned out to cheer their landing, including 1,200 civilian contract workers, 400 Marines of the 1st Defense Battalion Detachment under Major James Devereux, and the island commander, Navy Commander Winfield Cunningham. All that was missing was a brass band.

One of the pilots of VMF-211 was Captain Henry Talmadge Elrod, a big, large-boned man with an exuberant, outgoing personality marred only by occasional spells of moodiness. Elrod had an excess of energy which made him restless when stationary. It made him a bad desk man. It also made him an aggressive, hard-driving combat Marine whose pleasures were physical; he relished the sensation of flight, the taste of good food, the rough give and take of horseplay, the challenge of a noisy, elliptical argument. He was entertaining, straightforward, unafraid. His anger was explosive. According

10

to one of his squadron mates, he was very strong and capable of "a murderous passion."

Elrod was born in Turner County, Georgia, on September 27, 1905, the product of a rural, simple, easy-going society, but he was not altogether unlettered. He attended the University of Georgia—for a spell—and Yale College—for a spell. His restlessness with that sedentary life led him out of the academy and into the Marine Corps. "He was a man of action, a 'doer'," said Captain (now Major General) Frank Tharin. "As a Marine officer, he was dedicated to his profession." Elrod enlisted in 1927, became a second lieutenant in 1931 and, four years later, earned his wings. After tours of duty at the Quantico Marine Base and the San Diego Naval Air Station, he was assigned to the Hawaiian area in January, 1941. By the time he flew his Wildcat onto Wake, he was the Executive Officer of the squadron, a veteran pilot with considerable background in ground tactics as well; experience he was shortly to put to good use.

During the four peacetime days left to the men of Wake, social life, such as it was, centered on the southern leg of Wake Island, at the Officers' Club or about Camp II on the northern leg of the island, where civilian construction boss Dan Teeters had set up a general store, ice cream parlor and outdoor movie theatre. The Officers' Club, a small tent with a wooden floor, featured beer on ice, poker games, and interminable arguments, many of them set in motion by Elrod. "He would toss some provocative statement into the conversation," recalled Major Walter Bayler, "then defend it tooth and nail against criticism and attack."

11

Elrod was tall and well built, with a bluff, open face, a firm jawline and sensitive eyes. In repose, he seemed to be mulling over some vast, indefinable indignity, but these moments of subtle gloom were infrequent and rarely lasted long. Generally, he was hearty, extroverted, ready to amuse and be amused. On one occasion, he and Gunner Clarence McKinstry, a huge man six and a half feet tall, put on a wrestling match in the Officers' Club, grunting, crashing and tumbling half-naked across the unsanded floor like behemoths from a primitive age, until both burly men were exhausted, sated, and well-splintered. "Elrod," suggested Major Bayler dryly, "liked to take his pleasures the hard way."

On Monday morning, December 8 (which, east of the International Date Line, was Sunday, December 7) the dawn patrol flew off as usual on a scouting flight. Elrod, Lieutenants Carl Davidson and John Kinney and Technical Sergeant William Hamilton were the four pilots. Shortly after they disappeared into the overcast, the remainder of the squadron showed up for a breakfast of ham and eggs. Major Bayler finished his meal and stepped out, a minute or two before 7 A.M. He saw Major Devereux standing in front of his tent with a sheet of paper hanging limply from his hand. Devereux motioned Bayler to come closer.

"I've just had this message," he said calmly. "The Japs attacked Pearl Harbor this morning."

At Camp II, the civilian enclave, Commander Cunningham had also just finished his breakfast. The workers had reported to work at 7 A.M., as usual. Cunningham strolled out towards his pickup truck. It was a warm day and the surf was pounding, as it usually did, so heavily that he couldn't hear what the man running towards him from the radio shack was saying—though he was apparently shouting at the top of his voice. Gasping for breath, the man pushed a scrap of paper under his nose. "Pearl Harbor under attack, this is no drill, this is no drill," it said.

Cunningham's first thought was for the planes. He quickly went to his office, ordered the entire island to general quarters and contacted Putnam. They agreed between them that a constant four plane patrol should be maintained, with the remaining eight planes dispersed on the ground as far as possible. It was a decision Cunningham was to regret.

Moments later, construction boss Dan Teeters arrived wearing a steel helmet to offer his assistance and to announce that a number of the civilian workers wanted to sign up for military training.

The island, which, only moments earlier, had been basking in the soft laziness of a warm Pacific morning, suddenly was transformed into a hectic military garrison. Everywhere, trucks and jeeps raced along the sleek, white coral roads, some with no apparent purpose. Men, for the first time wearing full battle dress and the World War I pie plate helmets, and carrying ancient Springfield '03 rifles, ran to their battle stations. Ground crewmen trundled Wildcats to the edges of the airstrip—work had begun on protective bunkers, but these were not yet ready to receive the planes—then armorers took over and fed cartridge belts into the wing guns. Fuel trucks topped off the tanks. At the southeast corner of Wake, Devereux immediately set about organizing a command post.

By 7:35, all positions were manned. There were permanent 5-inch coastal guns at Peacock Point (Wake),

Toki Point (Peale), and Kuku Point (Wilkes) with 3-inch batteries augmenting them. There were .50-calibre antiaircraft machine guns and .30-calibre light machine guns sprinkled along the south shores of Wilkes and Wake, the east shore of Wake and the north shore of Peale, all facing seaward. At the Marine camp, atop a watertower, two men with field glasses scanned the skies to the south for approaching aircraft. There was no radar on Wake.

The Pan American clipper, which had taken off earlier that morning on its regular flight to Guam, came back and discharged its stunned passengers. Hastily pressed into service, its pilot began unloading cargo (airplane tires for British planes in Burma) in preparation for a long-range reconnaissance mission which he willingly agreed to carry out.

At 9 A.M., the dawn patrol returned for refueling, to learn for the first time that a state of war existed. Elrod took the news calmly. He had very little to say. He smoked a cigarette, drank a cup of coffee, and then took off again. Once in the air, he had his pilots clear their .50-calibre wing guns. The planes had no armor, nor did they have self-sealing fuel tanks, nor did any of the pilots have more than 30 hours logged with the new Wildcats. But it was too late to worry about any of that. The planes circled north of Wake, more or less ready for combat.

Throughout the morning, work proceeded amid a welter of excitement, anticipation and apprehension, though most of the servicemen were relatively calm. Many of the civilians were eager to pitch in. Many others decamped to the underbrush and couldn't be found—except that, shortly before noon, hunger pangs drove them to the dining halls.

It was at just about noon when 36 Japanese twin-engine bombers appeared from the south, flying in three elements of 12 planes each. The crashing surf effectively muted the roar of their engines and because the day was heavily overcast, they were practically over the island before they were spotted, at 11:50, by First Lieutenant William Lewis, Battery E Commander, at Peacock Point. Lewis started his 3-inch guns firing, but without effect. Two elements droned past the airfield to strike Camp II. The third element bombed the airstrip, then went on to attack the Pan American Hotel and seaplane ramps on Peale.

The entire raid lasted no more than fifteen minutes, but it was carried out skillfully and caused terrible damage and loss of life. Noiro Tsuji, observing from one of the bombers, noted that "the pilots in every one of the planes were grinning widely. Everyone waggled his wings to signify *banzai!*"

Most of the damage was suffered by VMF-211. Shortly before the bombers appeared, Bayler, Putnam, Captain Frank Tharin, Lieutenants George Graves, Frank Holden, Robert Conderman and Henry Webb had gathered outside a tent on the parking apron for some lunch. They were just about to go in when they saw the enemy planes, already crossing the shoreline at an altitude of about 3,000 feet. Immediately, they all began scattering.

Graves ran for his plane with the idea of going up to intercept. He jumped into the cockpit just as the first bombs struck. One of them was a direct hit on his Wild-cat. Killed instantly, Graves was thrown out, his body

15

landing under the right wing of his burning plane, and the flames set off the planes' 100-pound bombs and wing .50's, which added to the holocaust.

The other pilots raced south towards a patch of woods some 200 feet distant, but not all of them made it. Bombs were falling all about them. The earth shook. Hits on a 25,000-gallon tank of aviation gas set a fearful blaze going. Clouds of dense smoke obscured the airfield. Waves of intense heat scorched hair; concussion threatened to break eardrums. Three more Wildcats took direct hits, three others burst into flames and were destroyed. Of the eight planes on the ground, only one, badly damaged, survived the raid. Bayler's air-ground radio equipment was demolished. Tents were aflame throughout the area. A fuel truck and a number of 50-gallon drums were also burning fiercely.

When the bombers departed, the stunned survivors came out of cover to assess the damage. Putnam, bleeding slightly from a minor wound, was dazed and incredulous. He dragged behind him an old Springfield rifle, the stock of which had been shattered by machine gun fire. The squadron leader moved through the ruins of his base almost in a state of shock. Holden was lying on the runway, dead. Evidently he too had tried to reach a plane. Webb and Conderman, running only a few steps behind Bayler, failed to make the woods. Both were badly wounded. A Marine helped Bayler with an improvised litter to carry them away from the flames. Conderman, a red-headed and freckled youngster known as "Strawberry" was conscious and seemed the less hurt, though both his legs were fractured. "Be careful of those legs," he said quietly when they lifted him. He died that night in the contractor's hospital. Webb, badly pierced by shrapnel, seemed in worse shape, but he survived. In all, VMF-211 lost, of a total strength of 12 officers and 49 enlisted men, 3 officers and 20 enlisted men killed, 11 more wounded. Almost half of the ground crews had been wiped out.

By the time Cunningham got to the airport, Putnam had already begun to organize teams to fight fires and clear debris, but he was badly shaken. The news from Cunningham that many civilians, including five of Pan Am's Chamorro workers, had been killed, only deepened Putnam's rage. The Pan American base on Peale had been destroyed, but by the greatest bit of luck, the clipper itself, though holed, was able to fly. Within the hour it was on its way to Pearl Harbor with an overload of passengers, including all the Pan Am personnel.

The four Wildcats on patrol returned to a scene of devastation. Elrod, on landing his plane, plowed into a large junk pile of debris and bent his propellor, though fortunately the other three planes landed unscathed. The four pilots sprinted across the runway and checked in with Putnam, who gave them a quick résumé of the casualties. Elrod went to work helping the wounded onto trucks for transmittal to the contractor's hospital near Camp II.

Throughout the afternoon and evening, men worked feverishly to repair damage and to attempt to make the vital installations less vulnerable to bombardment. Some Marines and civilian contract workers loaded cases of .50-and .30-calibre ammunition onto trucks for distribution to guns and to burial holes on a parade ground, while others carted 3-inch shells from magazines to guns, dug foxholes, helped to construct bunkers for the surviving planes, carted food supplies to an assortment of camouflaged dumps, and dropped oil cans full of water all over the island, to be used as needed.

At the contractor's hospital, the civilian surgeon, Dr. Lawton Shank, and the Navy medical officer, Lieutenant (j.g.) Gustave Kahn, worked well into the morning hours operating on patients with gaping head wounds, with limbs nearly severed, with compound fractures, with internal bleeding; a grisly testimonial to the aerial bomb.

Early the following morning, VMF-211 had four planes in operation. Lieutenant Kinney and Technical Sergeant Hamilton were hard at work trying to salvage a fifth. Elrod and Frank Tharin had been assigned the job of preparing foxholes and defensive works in the squadron area south of the runway. The work wasn't made any easier by the knowledge that at any moment, they might be bombed.

As on the previous day, the Japanese bombers arrived shortly before noon. The raid that morning was not the surprise the first one had been. It was a clear, cloudless day, and from the water tower, Marine Gunner H. C. Borth gave the warning by phone and fired off a volley of three rifle shots, which was the only air alarm system the island had. Lieutenant David Kliewer and Technical Sergeant Hamilton, who were on patrol at the time, managed to intercept and knock down one of the bombers, but the remainder dropped their freight on a 3-inch gun, on Camp II, on the contractor's hospital (which had a large red cross painted on its roof), on civilian and Navy barracks, a garage, a blacksmith's shop, a large storehouse and a machine shop. When the enemy bombers turned around to go home, antiaircraft fire downed a second bomber, and five more were seen to be smoking. There was a good deal of cheering at the guns.

Casualties in VMF-211 were very light, but a large number of civilians and three wounded men in the hospital were killed. Lieutenant Webb, lying bandaged on his cot, had a close call: he reached out for a water pitcher and found it spouting water from bullet holes; he himself was untouched. Doctor Kahn had a similar experience. When the planes came over, he dived under a bed. Machine gun bullets ripped into the hospital and a pair of shoes sitting on the floor beside Kahn were shredded. The hospital, a wooden building, soon began burning, the patients and some of the medical equipment saved only by the efforts of the two doctors. Doctor Shank, though not in the service, subsequently was awarded a posthumous Navy Cross. (He was one of 98 civilians on Wake executed by the Japanese just prior to the American reoccupation of the island on September 4, 1945.)

The pattern of destruction fairly well convinced the island defenders that the enemy meant to occupy Wake after a suitable softening up period. The airfield runways had not been bombed, though the parked airplanes had. Neither had the power plant come under attack. Clearly, the Japanese hoped to have the use of these facilities when they arrived. The questions uppermost in the minds of the defenders were: When? How Soon?

The unequivocal response to this threat was a vigorous surge of energy: tending the wounded, digging still-useful objects out of ruined, smouldering heaps, moving undamaged guns to new locations and erecting dummy constructions in their place. Two concrete-reinforced, underground magazines were emptied of shells to serve as aid stations, a third for a communications center. Battery E moved from Peacock Point half a mile west to the woods south of the runway. In an underground hangar, Kinney and Hamilton exhausted themselves in a valiant effort to keep all operating aircraft functioning by "cannibalizing"—using parts taken from wrecked planes. Most of the defenders had a fairly realistic estimate of their chances, which were not terribly good; but all worked, and all listened eagerly for word of reinforcements. No such word came, though a relief expedition had already been conceived by Admiral Kimmel. However, a change in command, the state of near-paralysis brought on by the terrible damage suffered at Pearl Harbor, and a fear of adding to those losses were to result in fatal delays.

On the morning of December 10, another sunny, cloudless day, the Japanese raided Wake for the third time. Arriving at 10:45 ("They're early today," one Marine commented), the 26 Mitsubishi Zero-1 (Betty) bombers were first sighted by the Wildcat patrol, which was led that morning by Elrod. Elrod was seething with frustration. He had been on patrol north of the island at an elevation of 12,000 feet when the first raid occurred, but by the time his planes had rocketed down, the bombers were far out to sea. He hadn't been on patrol at the time of the second raid. His dull, restless anger was in part a result of his failure to mix with the enemy, in part a result of the propellor he had bent (which Kinney had already replaced). Elrod prided himself on his flying skill, and though the accident had been through no fault of his own, he was bothered. For all his flamboyance and easygoing grace, he set himself strict standards; it pained him not to meet them. He therefore felt a perverse gratitude when the Japanese bombers appeared, and eagerly led the four Wildcats into the enemy formation. In the scuffle that followed, Elrod shot down two of the Bettys. In Devereux's command post, a Marine watched Elrod slice into the bomber alignment and gloated, "Hammering Hank is sure giving it to them!" When he landed, Elrod was grinning happily and full of bounce once again.

The damage caused by the raid was negligible. The dummy guns at the position that Battery E had vacated were demolished and an ammunition dump on Wilkes had exploded, the blast killing one Marine and wounding four others. Two Battery L 5-inch guns at Kuku Point were warped, the fire control equipment shattered. Last and least, a number of frigate birds were wobbling about, dazed by the concussion.

Immensely heartened, the defenders were beginning to feel they could hold out indefinitely, even without reinforcements. The flyers, especially, were strutting, and with some justification. Like pilots the world over, they endlessly rehashed their flights and argued tactics. They agreed that altitude was essential, but the Japanese bombers, due to the accurate antiaircraft fire, were coming in higher and higher. This meant the Wildcats had to stay above them, in some cases without adequate supplies of oxygen, as the apparatus that normally refilled the bottles had never arrived on Wake. The problem was imaginatively solved by Captain Herbert Freuler, who rigged a transfer device that decanted Dan Teeter's supply of welding oxygen into the Wildcat containers. The danger of explosion was so great that each time he performed the operation, Freuler risked his life, yet he

21

A disabled F4F, photographed by Japanese after capturing Wake

never allowed anybody else to do it. Nevertheless, the supply of oxygen was low, and on one occasion, Elrod bounced out of his plane fuming bitterly. Without oxygen, he hadn't been able to press home an attack against the high-flying Betty bombers. He cursed and kicked at cans and vowed he wouldn't get caught low again no matter what the cost. Several days later, he climbed out of his cockpit looking decidedly under the weather.

"What's eating you?" Tharin asked.

Elrod grinned weakly. "I was flying around up there without oxygen. The whole time. And," he added unconvincingly, "I may just do it again."

The invasion attempt, which everybody on Wake had long since known was inevitable, came on the morning of December 11. Nine warships of Rear Admiral Sadamichi Kajioka's landing force left Roi Island in the Marshalls on December 9, escorting transports *Kongo Maru* and *Konryu Maru*, which carried some 450 Japanese Marines. The convoy made its landfall by 3 A.M. on the eleventh. The seas were heavy and the wind high. The island lay in darkness. Not a light shone. Not a gun fired. The Japanese were quite convinced there would be no undue resistance. A press release, in fact, had already been prepared for Radio Tokyo announcing the capture of Wake Island. Still, Kajioka approached the island warily. By 5 A.M., the flagship cruiser *Yubari* was about 9,000 yards south of Peacock Point. Dawn was breaking. The ships were clearly visible in the morning haze, yet no guns fired. Could the defenders have been annihilated? Not likely. *Yubari* and two other cruisers started a run broadside and fired 6-inch shells, setting fire to diesel oil tanks. Still there was no answering fire. The cruisers turned eastward, made another firing run, then turned west again. They were then no more than 4,000 to 5,000 yards offshore, due south of Peacock Point, where Battery A, commanded by First Lieutenant Clarence Barninger, patiently trained its 5-inch coastal guns and waited for the order to fire. At 6:15, the order came.

Three hours earlier, Commander Cunningham had been awakened by Gunner John Hamas, who reported sighting the invasion fleet. One of the batteries at Kuku Point had requested permission to illuminate with searchlights. Cunningham said no. The island defenders were surely outgunned, Cunningham reasoned. Their best hope lay in luring the Japanese cruisers and destroyers to point-blank range.

With mounting impatience, the gunners waited out

the shelling. Many thought the order to withhold fire insane. At Devereux's command post, one Marine was heard to mutter, "What the hell are we supposed to do, wait until they climb on our backs?"

At Peacock Point, Barninger tracked *Yubari*.

At Kuku Point, Second Lieutenant John McAlister tracked several destroyers approaching Wilkes.

In the VMF-211 area, the pilots scrambled out of their foxholes. Putnam, Freuler, Tharin and Elrod were ready to take off, but Devereux asked them to wait until the shelling started. They fretted with the delay.

Nobody slept. Every man was at his battle station and, as the sky lightened, and the visible shapes of warships were outlined by the rising sun, tension mounted steadily. At his command post, Cunningham stared at his watch, his muscles aching, a knot of anxiety in his belly.

"They're getting closer," somebody said. "An awful lot of them."

At 6:15, Cunningham's "talker" held out the phone. Cunningham grabbed it.

Gunner Hamas was on the other end, reporting that the Japanese ships had closed to 4,600 yards and that batteries at both Points were sighted in.

"Okay," Cunningham said, taking a deep breath. "Cut loose at them, John!"

Barninger's first rounds landed over. He came down 500. *Yubari* fired two salvos, several hundred yards over, then 100 yards short, but it was Barninger who drew first blood, with four hits on *Yubari's* hull and one on a turret. The shells were being passed by civilian John Burroughs to civilian John Clelan to Sergeant Tony

Poulousky who kept muttering for them to speed it up. Batteries on Kuku and Toki Points soon joined in. The Japanese ships broke formation. The transports headed out to sea, while the destroyers steamed west of Kuku Point, came under fire of the Toki Point guns, and one of them was hit. Still in formation, they turned southwest. At 6:50, McAlister's Battery L hit destroyer *Hayate*, which broke in two, sinking in less than two minutes with no survivors.

The effect of this sight on the gunners at Kuku Point was invigorating. They jumped up and down, hugged each other and hooted like wild men; all except an old China hand, Platoon Sergeant Henry Bedell, who growled with disgust, "Knock it off, and get back on the guns. What do you think this is, a ball game?"

Chastened, the gunners of Love Battery got back on the guns and promptly hit the destroyer *Oite*, one of the transports, and one of the three cruisers.

Able Battery hit one of two patrol boats and from the northernmost point on Peale, Baker's 5-inch guns scored on destroyer *Yayoi*. Kajioka was convinced. At 7 A.M., he ordered a general retreat to Kwajalein, and ten minutes later the ships were all beyond the range of Wake's guns; though not beyond the range of her Wildcats.

As soon as the shore batteries ceased fire, Putnam, Elrod, Tharin and Freuler took off, as excited as young boys. Even the usually undemonstrative Putnam could hardly contain himself. As squadron commander, he shouldn't have been flying; but he wasn't going to miss the show for anything. Within minutes the Wildcats sighted the convoy. They dipped their wings and came down in the face of antiaircraft fire to drop their 100-

pound bombs, and strafe with their wing guns. Fighter pilots of World War II were notorious chatterers, repeated admonitions from squadron leaders to shut up notwithstanding, and Elrod and Tharin were no exceptions. Bayler, sitting by the ground-air communications, heard them carrying on:

"Hiee! Right in the skipper's lap!"

"Ooops, there goes her magazine."

"My guns are jammed." Short pause. "I'm going down *anyway.*"

With their bombs expended, they scorched in for a landing, refueled and rearmed, and went up again. "Up-sydaisy," Elrod chortled. He and Tharin were having a marvelous time, and in addition were scoring hits. While they were battering light cruisers *Tenryu* and *Tatsuta*, Freuler was dropping an egg on the stern of *Kongo Maru.* Flames blossomed. The pilots crowed. Putnam and Freuler came back and gave Kinney and Hamilton a turn. In all, the shuttle made 10 sorties, dropping 20 bombs and using up 20,000 rounds of .50-calibre ammo. Elrod, at one point, thought he had planted one of his bombs in the smokestack of destroyer *Kisaragi*, but to his great disappointment there was only a dim muffled explosion. A few minutes later, at 7:31, Kinney was pushing over to hit the destroyer and she blew up in his face, the victim of Elrod's "dud," which had finally set off below-decks depth charges. Elrod thus became the first pilot of the war to sink a warship with small bombs.

The Japanese conceded after the war that the Wake Island fiasco was one of the most humiliating defeats their Navy had ever suffered. Assessments of Japanese losses subsequently ranged as high as nine ships and

5,000 men (these were the figures Devereux favored), but in point of fact, only two destroyers sank, with a loss of life estimated by Japanese military historian Captain Tashikazu Ohmae at "nearly 500." This was victory enough, considering that Wake suffered only four Marines wounded, none killed. It was to be the only time during the entire course of the war that shore guns repelled an invasion fleet. The defense was well conceived and brilliantly executed by men who were, for the most part, inexperienced recruits in their first action; and the civilians, rank amateurs, had learned their tasks in only three days. At Battery A, Sergeant Poulousky grinned cagily at Burroughs and Clelan. "You civilians are okay," he admitted gruffly. He shook hands with them, and everybody beamed with pride.

The celebration was marred moments later by the loss of two Wildcats, the Japanese antiaircraft fire having scored heavily on the unarmored fighters. Freuler's oil cooler and one cylinder had been pierced. Elrod heard him say, "My engine's hit," and saw him dropping down towards the runway. Freuler made it, but the engine was a dead loss. Elrod himself had suffered worse damage. After his last pass, his main fuel line was holed and the plane began to wobble, losing altitude rapidly. Elrod tried to fight it, but the Wildcat plunged lower and lower. On the ground, Bayler, Putnam and Devereux, among others, saw the plane sinking and raced across the coral road and down towards the beach. "It seemed certain he would never make the island," Devereux recalled. Bayler was sure he would smash into the foaming surf, but Elrod fought the downward pull and coaxed a few extra feet of altitude. The Wildcat cleared the water by no more than three or four feet and pancaked onto the beach amid a spray of sand, coral and rock. When the tearing, wrenching sounds stopped, the stubby fighter lay telescoped, a clump of twisted fabric and steel, an utter wreck. Elrod was shaken and had a small cut on his cheek but was otherwise unhurt. He climbed out of the cockpit, shook his head and patted the plane sadly. Devereux and Putnam came running up. Elrod seemed more embarrassed than anything else. "I'm sorry about the plane," he said. He had a guilty look on his face. "Honest, I'm awful sorry about it."

"You just sank a Jap cruiser," Devereux said.

"It wasn't your fault," Putnam said.

Elrod looked morose. All the way back to the runway, he kept apologizing as though it were his fault, and soon afterwards he disappeared. He didn't want to hear the others tell him what a great job of flying it had been just to get as far as the beach. That would only have pained him more.

At 10 A.M., the land-based Betty bombers from Roi came over, as usual, and were met by Davidson and Kinney in the two remaining Wildcats. Davidson had promised himself two kills, one each for Conderman and Holden, and this personal animus powered his reckless attacks. Davidson got his two, and Kinney sent another one home trailing billows of smoke, a probable kill, considering that the distance to Roi was 620 miles. Davidson was in ecstasy when he landed. "We were assaulted by a gibbering maniac who appeared to be hysterical," Bayler noted. Davidson was babbling, "I got 'em, I got em; I said I would and I did," and hurling himself onto everybody in sight.

Late in the afternoon, receivers tuned in to Radio

28

Tokyo heard the young lady later to be nicknamed Tokyo Rose cheerily announce the fall of Wake Island. Evidently Admiral Kajioka hadn't yet been able to notify Combined Fleet to cancel the previously arranged press release. For the Marines who heard the announcement, it was an amusing end to a day of high achievements.

During the week that followed, the Roi bombers came almost daily in squadrons of 23 to 33 planes. These raids were augmented, periodically, by Kawanishi-97 flying boats arriving just before dawn or just at dusk. Tharin downed one of these on the twelfth. That same day, Kinney rehabilitated a third Wildcat, but on the thirteenth, Freuler washed out in order to avoid hitting a crane which was inexplicably sitting beside the runway, and the plane was wrecked. On the fourteenth, the Bettys scored a direct hit on one of the two surviving Wildcats. Kinney, Hamilton and Aviation Machinist Mate 1/C James Hesson, who had joined the repair party, rushed into the hangar and, while the Wildcat burned fiercely, calmly removed the engine, which was still intact. They then set to work accumulating spare parts, worked unceasingly and, somehow, by 6 A.M. on the seventeenth, had three Wildcats in use. At noon, when the Bettys arrived and the squadron went up to intercept, one washed out on takeoff, and the marvellous mechanics, for all their obsessive tinkering, were never able to put a third one in the air from that day until the end came.

Relief rumors, during that week, had all but ceased. The defenders were pretty well convinced they had been deserted. Cunningham repeatedly sent calls for help and received back such irrelevancies as a query on the progress of the lagoon-dredging operation—which had necessarily been discontinued as of December 8—and the suggestion, "If you lack glass to put in barracks windows, seismograph paper excellent substitute." Perhaps the most maddening communication received from Pearl Harbor advised, "All personnel will wear long trousers and keep sleeves rolled down as protection against bomb blasts."

The Marines, needless to say, needed no such paternal cluckings. They had long since learned that a man's chances of surviving an air raid were good if he could get to a bunker or sandbagged foxhole before the bombs fell. Some of the personnel shelters, in time, took on fairly livable dimensions. Elrod and Tharin shared one which boasted its own sandbagged revetment, an entryway, and a pantry which consisted of five 5-gallon water cans and a larder of twelve tins of food. Since excessive movement was discouraged during midday, lunch was generally a cold affair of hardtack and jam, but Dan Teeters had fixed up a galley in a truck which made the rounds for breakfast and dinner. The menu was unvarying (stew, bread and coffee) but it was hot and nourishing, and very welcome.

In the evening, the pilots gathered at the CP to trade gossip and banter in a sardonic, not so lighthearted way about their situation, which clearly was deteriorating. Most felt in some degree betrayed, and Elrod felt especially bitter. One afternoon he stormed into Devereux's quarters in a rage.

"Why on earth doesn't somebody come out and help us fight?" he fumed. Devereux could only shrug his shoulders helplessly.

The relief expedition was, in fact, on the way. Accompanied by three cruisers and a destroyer squadron, the carrier *Saratoga,* carrying Marine Fighter Squadron 221 with 18 Wildcats, departed Pearl Harbor on December 16. The much slower oiler *Neches* and seaplane tender *Tangier,* carrying supplies, ammunition and equipment, had left a day earlier on the 2,100 mile journey. At the same time, Admiral Halsey's *Enterprise* task group steamed for Johnston Island, as a standby support force. The first word that the island defenders had of this expedition came on Saturday, December 20, when a Navy PBY casually landed in the lagoon as though no war were in progress and delivered the long awaited message. Cunningham was advised to prepare to receive aircraft and to have the civilians ready to be evacuated by the twenty-fourth—a splendid Christmas present indeed.

The news electrified the Marines, who were, by then, down to two badly scarred fighters and only one battery of 3-inch AA guns able to fire; everything else had been destroyed or damaged by the air raids, including practically every building and structure on the island. Almost without exception, the men were exhausted, with stubbled cheeks and sunken, red-rimmed eyes. When they heard that they hadn't been forgotten after all, many shaved, a gesture that implied new hope, and nobody seemed quite as tired.

When the PBY took off early Sunday morning with Major Bayler, the "last man off Wake," aboard, the relief expedition was only 600 miles from Wake. There seemed no reason why they couldn't arrive within two days at most, yet they never did arrive. Caution and confusion had marked the progress of the convoy from the first, and when on December 21, 18 Japanese Type-99 (Val) bombers with an escort of 18 Zero-3 (Zeke) fighters swarmed over Wake, American timidity increased. Since the short range Zekes could not have come from a land base, they must have come from carriers.

There were, in fact, several Japanese task groups in the area. They had been detached from Vice Admiral Chuichi Nagumo—who was then returning from the Pearl Harbor attack—in order to support Kajioka's second invasion attempt. One was a cruiser division under Rear Admiral Hiroake Abe. Another was a carrier division, built around carriers *Hiryu* and *Soryu,* both of which would later be sunk at Midway. It was from these carriers, commanded by Rear Admiral Tamon Yamaguchi—a graduate of Princeton University—that the Zekes had come.

Admiral Chester Nimitz had replaced Kimmel as Commander, Pacific Fleet, but he was still stateside, and Vice Admiral William Pye, temporarily in command, feared Yamaguchi's carriers. Pye didn't want to present his new boss with the news that *Saratoga* had been sunk by their planes. The entire night of December 21, the worried admiral discussed with his staff what course to take, and at 9:11 the following morning, he ordered *Saratoga* back to Pearl Harbor. According to Halsey, when pilots of VMF-221 heard that they wouldn't be allowed to fly off *Sara's* deck to relieve Wake, they sat down and cried. On the bridge, Rear Admiral Aubrey Fitch was begged by angry staff officers to disobey the order. The talk eventually became so mutinous that Fitch departed so as not to hear it; he himself felt exactly the same way.

That same morning, at 10 A.M., 33 Type-97 (Kate) bombers and six Zekes from *Hiryu* and *Soryu* arrived for the sixteenth and final air raid of the Wake campaign. They were met by Freuler and Davidson. Young Davidson piled in eagerly. At one point, Freuler saw him dog-fighting with a pair of Zekes, and that was the last anyone saw of Davidson. Freuler smoked one Zeke and fired into a second, which immediately blew up in his face and scorched his Wildcat. He twisted his plane in search of Davidson, and while he was thus occupied, another Zeke got on his tail and hurled several rounds into the cockpit. The Wildcat immediately went sluggish, the manifold pressure dropped; ailerons and stabilizers were shredded. Freuler himself was hit by two .60-calibre slugs. Somehow, he managed to evade the Zeke. He had lost a great deal of blood and he was feeling faint, but he hung on and, after making four passes over the field while Bettys continued to bomb it, he crash-landed. They found him unconscious, blood-soaked, with a hunk of flesh missing from his shoulder.

VMF-211 was out of business. Kinney, with no more planes to patch up, promptly collapsed. At the hospital, the diagnosis was "severe diarrhea and exhaustion." The remainder of the pilots reported for duty as ground troops. One group, under Major Putnam, collected around a 3-inch gun which was being manned by Lieutenant Robert Hanna and civilians Robert Bryan, Eric Lehtola and Paul Gay. None of the civilians knew anything about guns. North of them, across the coral road, another group under Elrod and Tharin, also including a number of civilians, dug in as skirmishers. There they waited. The night was moonless, utterly dark, and quiet save for the incessant pounding of the surf. At about 1

A.M., December 23, a number of flares began puffing into brilliance against the black sky. Several machine guns along the defense perimeter started up nervously. A searchlight went on, angry voices shouted and a moment later, it flicked off. From the ships at sea, beams of light spun out, crossed each other's paths, and the red flares fizzled out in descending wiggles. At first, the defenders hoped this might be their relief.

Shortly, it became apparent that it was the second Japanese invasion attempt.

At Hanna's gun, which was to be the center of the bitterest fighting, the motley skirmishers prepared for the blow. Hanna cut powder bags and fuses for the shortest possible burst. The gun had no sights for direct laying, so Hanna zeroed in "Kentucky" fashion by peering through the breech and cranking the gun until it pointed at one of two dim shapes slowly approaching the beach. These were patrol boats 33 and 34, carrying three companies under Lieutenants Uchida, Takano and Itaya. Hanna patiently held his fire and was rewarded when one of the landing craft, inexplicably, turned on a hooded searchlight. Hanna quickly swiveled his gun and fired. His second round hit the boat's magazine; small arms, grenades and shells began exploding. The boat burst into flames. With the help of this light, Hanna took the second boat under fire, hitting it several times. The two boats yawed in the surf, and went out of control. Men jumped off into four or five feet of water, some of them drowning, others struggling ashore and falling onto the beach.

The skirmishers began firing at them with Browning automatic rifles, Thompson submachine guns, rifles, pistols, and one or two .30-calibre machine guns. The tracers flew out like rivets to spatter against the sand and coral. The enemy wore gas masks on their backs, and many of them were pierced or carried away by the firing. Slowly, the enemy crept forward under the fusillade.

At the same time, Japanese barges had landed troops farther to the west, at the channel between Wake and Wilkes and at Kuku Point. Other enemy troops, in rubber boats, paddled into the lagoon and landed on the inner shoreline, thus setting up an encirclement of the Marine positions. Fire fights erupted all over the southern shore. Telephone lines were cut and confusion soon turned the battle into a series of disconnected local encounters. Cunningham, at Camp II, had no way to control the fight, nor did Devereux. The local commanders were on their own. Cunningham sent to Pearl Harbor at 2:50 A.M.: ISLAND UNDER GUNFIRE. ENEMY APPARENTLY LANDING. He dispatched some men from Peale to the south shore of Wake, then tried in vain to figure out what was going on. He could see tracers flying through the air, but couldn't tell who was doing the shooting. At 5 A.M. he sent: THE ENEMY IS ON THE ISLAND. THE ISSUE IS IN DOUBT.

South of the runway, in the gnarled scrub, the issue was gradually resolving itself. Several hundred Japanese Marines were assailing a handful of men under Putnam, Elrod and Tharin. Part of the Uchida Detachment had crawled to within 20 yards of the skirmishers and prepared to charge. A hail of grenades burst among them. They charged. The Marine guns opened up and Elrod, in a murderous frenzy, jumped up with his tommy gun,

35

firing and swearing. Among others, Lieutenant Uchida fell with a bullet in his forehead. A Japanese survivor recalled this moment: "One large figure appeared before us to blaze away with a machine gun from his hips as they do in American gangster films." The American defenders were "huge shadows" which "shouted something unintelligible"—certainly something unprintable. The Japanese charge was broken, some of the first wave having fallen at Elrod's feet, close enough for him to touch. As the enemy retreated, the Marines kept firing and screaming bloody oaths. Then things quieted down momentarily. The assault wave turned up the beach and moved across the road west of Hanna's gun to disappear into the brush. Grenades from manually operated launchers popped up in a high trajectory and began raining down on the Marine positions. Putnam's group, exposed south of the road, tried to join Elrod's group in the brush, but a machine gun drove them back. Two civilians took cover in an overturned AA carrier and were killed by mortars. At Hanna's gun, Bryan and Gay were killed, Lehtola injured. A Japanese rifleman fired at Putnam. The round hit a 3-inch shell and ricocheted off with an elongated whine. Hanna fired his .45 pistol and killed the sniper. Putnam had been wounded earlier; he'd been hit in the jaw. From time to time he passed out, rejoining the fight when he regained consciousness. The few survivors at his position finally made it safely across the road and into the brush, joining Elrod and Tharin. "This is as far as we go," Putnam gasped.

At 6:30, Cunningham sent the last dispatch that was to come out of Wake: ISLAND RINGED WITH SHIPS. Surrender came an hour later.

36

Just before daylight, Elrod, Tharin and a few others had worked around to the west, crawling through a field of dead Japanese bodies. They spread out and prepared to throw back the next rush. Off to their side, a clump of supposedly dead enemy soldiers began creeping forward. Elrod had just popped up to hurl a hand grenade when this group began firing. Elrod pitched forward. Tharin swiveled and knocked off the infiltrators with his tommy gun, then ran to Elrod's side, to see what he could do.

Because of the faulty communications, it turned out to be more difficult to surrender than expected. A number of Marines refused to heed the order. Devereux finally had to rig a white flag and go from position to position to get the firing to stop. When he reached Hanna's gun, he found only ten men still alive, and of these only Tharin wasn't wounded. These ten had been holding off several hundred enemy troops. They threw their guns down wearily and stumbled out of the brush. Putnam came forward, his face a red smear, and a dazed, sorrowful look clouding his features. He said to Devereux, "Jimmy, I'm sorry, poor Hank is dead."

That afternoon, Admiral Kajioka came ashore wearing full dress whites with ribbons strung across his chest and a dress sword hanging from his waist. In a formal ceremony, he took possession of the island for the Emperor. The American flag, which had been flying continuously since December 8, came down, and the Japanese flag went up. The name of the island changed: Wake was rechristened Otori Shima, which means Bird Island.

37

Sergeant Mitchell Paige (after his promotion to lieutenant)

2

THE NIGHT THE FIREFLIES ATTACKED

~~~~~~

PLATOON SERGEANT MITCHELL PAIGE

"H" Company, 7th Marines

OCTOBER 24-26, 1942

Following the loss of Wake Island, Hong Kong and Singapore fell, Bataan and Corregidor fell, and the Japanese completed their conquest of Burma. A series of naval engagements in the Java Sea ended March 1, with fire from an enemy cruiser sinking the destroyer *Pope*, the last Allied ship in those waters. The Japanese Navy was, by early May, in complete control of the Indian Ocean, the South China Sea, the Java Sea, the Celebes Sea, the Philippine Sea and much of the Pacific Ocean.

Having completed the first phase of her military operations without a setback, Japan turned her attention to Australia and the Solomon Islands. The occupation of Florida, Tulagi and Guadalcanal in the Solomons was followed, on May 7, by an attempt to capture Port Moresby on the southeast tip of New Guinea. The ensuing Battle of the Coral Sea was in itself indecisive, but it did cause the cancellation of the Port Moresby assault, and for this reason can be counted an American "victory," the first of the war.

Even more significant was the Battle of Midway, on June 3-6. The Japanese defeat, and their loss for the first time of major warships (aircraft carriers *Akagi, Kaga, Soryu* and *Hiryu* and cruiser *Mikuma* sunk) suggested the possibility that the Imperial Japanese Navy was not altogether invincible. The effect on morale in the United States was as invigorating as it was demoralizing in Japan, where some high staff officers recognized the battle to have been a pivotal one. Japanese fortunes, from Midway on, took a turn for the worse.

One direct consequence of the crucial victory was that Japanese plans for further adventures in distant waters were laid aside. In their place was substituted, according to Masotake Okumiya, a "new, curving defense line which was to be held at virtually all costs before an enemy who was now expected to commence his own assault operations." One of the outposts of this perimeter was the island of Guadalcanal.

"Guadalcanal. A name, merely a name. We did not even know what Guadalcanal was: an island, a military base, a secret operation code name, perhaps. When the American forces stormed ashore at Guadalcanal, we had never even heard of the island." So wrote Flight Petty Officer, 1/C, Saburo Sakai, top surviving Japanese flying ace, in a battle log.

The anonymous island, at the southeast end of the Solomons chain, had great strategic importance. In Jap-

40

anese hands, it threatened supply routes to New Guinea where a protracted land battle was being fought and, in consequence, would continue to endanger not only Port Moresby, but all of Australia as well. During the summer of 1942, Japanese planners decided to strengthen Guadalcanal. American planners decided to assault it. Thus was drawn the crucial six-month-long campaign that began on August 7, 1942, when the 1st Marine Division under Major General Alexander Vandegrift landed on the island, swept inland almost without resistance and captured an airfield the Japanese had only recently constructed. Renamed Henderson Field, in honor of Major Lofton Henderson, a Marine aviator who had been killed at the Battle of Midway, the airbase was to prove the prize for which some 31,000 American and Japanese lives were lost.

Henderson lay in the north-central portion of the island, bounded on three sides by dense rain forest and on the north by Sealark Channel. The jungles, heavily overgrown, supported many hundreds of different species of insects, spiders and ants, each more repellent than the next. There were taro leaves the shape and size of a mastodon's ear, innumerable ferns, banana trees with sharp, irregular leaves, hardwood giants rising to a height of 100 feet or more, and an exotic suffusion of tropical plants, vines, creepers and flowers, all of them tangled together to form a nearly impenetrable barrier. A dank, sickly sweet odor hung over the jungle, which the constant fall of rain kept soggy and humid. As far as the men who had to fight there were concerned, it was an unhappy arena for combat.

The earliest battles were drawn to the east of the airfield, at the Tenaru River, and at Tasimboko and Taivu Villages. The first Japanese counterblow was the landing of Colonel Kiyono Ichiki's detachment of 900 men at Taivu on August 18. This force assaulted the 1st Marine Regiment lines at the Tenaru River and was destroyed. Colonel Ichiki, having predicted victory in his diary, was mortified in the extreme and shot himself in the head.

Following this, a 5,000-man brigade under Major General Kiyotake Kawaguchi landed at Tasimboko. The general had brought a pair of dress whites along with him, which he meant to wear when he accepted the American commander's sword, but Lieutenant Colonel Merritt "Red Mike" Edson's Raiders overwhelmed Kawaguchi's supply train and captured the uniform. Four days later, on September 12, 2,000 men of the Kawaguchi brigade attacked at a place called Bloody Ridge, only to be beaten back by Edson's undermanned battalion of Marines. Kawaguchi lost large numbers of men in the attack and many more during the retreat westward through the jungles. The general was lucky to keep his own sword.

The scene of battle shifted, at this stage, to west of the airfield. In the Kukum Hills, Lieutenant Colonel Lewis "Chesty" Puller won a battle which extended the Marine lines west to the Matanikau River; following which, Puller, Edson and Colonel "Wild Bill" Whaling combined forces to annihilate the newly-landed 4th Regiment of the Sendai 2nd Division in the Matanikau-Point Cruz area.

Despite these terrible losses, the enemy still held the upper hand. Admiral Chester Nimitz admitted that

Japan controlled the seas and that "our supply of the positions will only be done at great expense." There was no hope of reinforcements for the weary, malaria-ridden men of the 1st Marine Division. Japanese reinforcements, however, continued to pour onto the island; by mid-October it was clear to General Vandegrift that his opposite number, 17th Army commander Lieutenant General Haruyoshi Hyakutate, was building towards another climactic engagement.

The Marine lines, at the time, ran west and south of Henderson Field, roughly in the shape of a pair of shallow bowls connected by a spoon laid across them. On the left (eastern) flank was Puller's 1st Battalion, 7th Marines, supported by the Army's 164th Regiment. In the center were the 5th Marines, and the 1st Marines minus a battalion. All these troops faced south and southwest. On the extreme right flank, facing west to the Matanikau River, was the 3rd Battalion, 7th Marines. Behind them, a series of east-west ridges were undefended.

When, on the afternoon of October 24, a large body of Japanese troops were observed tramping their way east, south of the 3rd Battalion's open-ended and unsupported left flank, General Vandegrift hastily sent the 2nd Battalion, 7th Marines, under Colonel Herman Hanneken, to fill the gap.

Easy Company of Hanneken's battalion, facing south, occupied the portion of the ridge line farthest west, tieing in to the 3rd Battalion's exposed left flank. Then came George Company, and farthest east was Fox Company. Between George and Fox was a protruding knoll, the defense of which was assigned to a machine gun platoon from How (Heavy Weapons) Company, led by

43

Platoon Sergeant Mitchell Paige, a dark-haired, boyish looking, twenty-four-year-old. In the battle that ensued, the Japanese struck most heavily at the ridges south of Henderson, where Puller's battalion was emplaced, and west of Henderson, at the knoll manned by Paige's platoon, a force of roughly 30 men.

Sergeant Paige, a professional Marine, did not smoke or drink. He was a quiet man, not given to unruly outbursts of temper, and his most vehement oath, reserved for the enemy, was "damned slopehead," which, among any body of fighting men, would be considered a decidedly puny effort. Although he did not consider himself a religious man, he nevertheless by his own account "carried a Bible all the time" when he was overseas. Prior to Pearl Harbor, he had served tours of duty in China, the Philippines and Cuba. In his six years in the service, he had won a reputation for being a sturdy, soft-spoken, knowledgeable Marine non-com.

He had originally attempted to enlist in the Marine Corps in July, 1936, at the age of seventeen. On being told that he had not yet reached the minimum age, he retired to await the necessary passage of time, appearing once again at the Baltimore Recruiting Office on August 31, his eighteenth birthday. A shy, mild-mannered youngster, he had spent three years at McKeesport High School, McKeesport, Pennsylvania without distinguishing himself either as an especially good or bad student, nor had he participated in the life of the school. As he lived in Camden, a distance away, he knew few of his fellow students or teachers well. He spent much of his spare time playing semi-professional football with a team known as the Dravosburg Firemen.

"Most of the players were old men," Paige recalled. "I was the only kid." They were not, in fact, especially old, nor was he very much of a kid. He was, emotionally, more in contact with his mature teammates than with his schoolmates, and he gravitated to the Marine Corps expecting to find much of the same companionship, and the challenge of a service life; though perhaps not as much of a challenge as he was to face on Guadalcanal the night of October 26, 1942.

Hanneken's battalion left the airfield just before dawn on the twenty-fourth, moving to bolster the undefended high ground behind (to the east of) the 3rd Battalion, 7th Marines. They were, during this move, under observation of enemy field pieces. The passage through the dense jungles, up onto spiny ridges, back down to the jungle, then up again to the next ridge, was not only wearying; it was accompanied by frequent interdicting barrages of artillery and mortar fire, and as a result, the ten-mile trip ate up all the daylight hours. Just at dusk, battalion headquarters set up its command post at the base of the rear slope; the three rifle companies, each accompanied by its assigned machine gun platoon from How Company, trudged wearily up the last hillside.

Paige's men came up to their new position in darkness, the evening of October 24, going slowly and carefully along the winding trail but stumbling anyway on tangled roots, and losing their footing in the boggy turf under the umbrella of tall hardwoods, lush tropical giants that incessantly dripped rain. The ridge, on top, was grass, but hard as cement underneath. Nobody had strength enough left to dig himself a foxhole.

Before they were able to set up their guns, the drizzle turned into a heavy downpour. The men were bone-weary, wet, chilled and miserable, and visibility was very poor. It was so bad that Paige wasn't even sure they'd reached the nose of the ridge. He had to crawl on the ground and grope his way forward by hand. When he reached out and felt the ridge dropping away on all sides, he turned and told his men, "We're here. Let's get the guns set up."

After emplacing the platoon's .30-calibre water-cooled heavy machine guns and arranging a security watch, Paige gathered his men and distributed a meagre ration of Spam by scooping the meat out of the can with his fingers and dropping each man's portion into his outstretched hand. There also was to have been a can of peaches which had been "borrowed" from some rear echelon stores but the man entrusted with it had stumbled in the darkness and dropped the can down the forward slope of the ridge.

"I was too scared to tell you about it," the man stuttered, stoically accepting the round of abuse the others heaped on his head. He could not himself recall ever having committed a worse crime.

After chow, the men dispersed to their guns. Paige periodically called their names to make sure they were awake and, sometime after midnight, crawled forward to the edge of the knoll. There, with the rain pelting his face, he lay on his back. It helped keep him alert and allowed him to scan the sky for enemy flares, planes and star shells—a habit that continual enemy air raids and naval bombardments had fostered. It also involved less expenditure of energy in that position to turn his head and press an ear to the ground to improve his hearing. Paige listened intently for sounds of enemy activity.

It was so dark that nothing existed save what could be heard or felt. The predominant emotion was loneliness and an overwhelming sense of isolation. In that black cave of night, the only reality was the rain drenching them and the knowledge that, somewhere in the jungle, other men meant to kill them.

At about 2 A.M., Paige was startled into a charged wakefulness by what were, unmistakably, low mumbling sounds. He woke up Pfc "Smitty" Smith, and together they strained their ears. A few minutes later, they heard the same sounds again. Paige was able to pick out a word or two of Japanese.

He quickly scurried from man to man, warning them to stand by for enemy action, then returned to the listening post, his mind racing. He had no idea how large a force was out in front of him, or where precisely they were. Exposing his position by opening fire would not be wise; but then neither would sitting back and letting the Japanese infiltrate the perimeter. They might, at that moment, already be preparing to charge. Paige resolved his indecision by taking action.

"Let's get this over with right now," he said hoarsely, not entirely sure he was doing the right thing. He pulled a pin from a grenade and dropped it over the edge. As soon as his men heard the click, they followed suit with a cascade of grenades. There were a number of muffled explosions. There were also screams of pain. With Smitty pulling the pins, Paige hurled a few more grenades; then silence descended on the jungle, and that was the end of it. A small Japanese reconnaissance patrol had made contact with a Marine outpost; a minor skirmish, but one which was clearly a prelude to a more vigorous contest.

The only sound for the rest of the night was the lulling spatter of rain, but the tension, the fear and the galling discomfort kept most of the men awake. In the morning, while they were cutting foxholes into the ridge—they had no entrenching tools, so they used their bayonets—several men from George Company came over to complain about the noise of the night before.

"What are you guys, trigger-happy?" one non-com groused. "You men dumb rookies, or what?"

The accusations, understandably, riled Paige's men, some of whom were ready for a fight anyway. There was a good deal of growling and fussing that was finally stopped only by the appearance of Major Odell Conoley, the battalion's executive officer, who had come up the reverse slope from battalion headquarters to investigate the disturbance. Paige showed him the bodies of two dead enemy soldiers lying at the base of the forward slope, and pointed out large pools of blood in the draw plus several trails of blood leading back into the jungle, where 15 more Japanese bodies lay.

Major Conoley nodded his head judiciously.

He said: "Sergeant, you better get your men some more grenades."

The implied compliment, clearly, vindicated Paige's judgment.

Throughout the daylight hours of October 25, Paige's platoon tended its weapons and waited with some apprehension for night to fall. All that day, the Imperial Japanese Navy sent destroyers down from Rabaul to shell Marine installations; there were also numerous dogfights between Zeroes and Wildcats. Marines spent so much time diving for cover they thereafter remembered October 25 as "Dugout Sunday." The one joyous moment of the day for Paige's platoon came when a reconnaissance patrol returned with a heartwarming "contact" report: the lost can of peaches had been found. It was quickly gobbled up. After the orgy, the platoon settled down to more waiting. They did not yet know that for them, battle was imminent; that reports received at Battalion C.P. indicated a strong Japanese force had engaged the 1st Battalion, 7th Marines some 2,000 yards south of Henderson the night before.

This was the main thrust of the Japanese assault, mounted by Lieutenant General Masao Maruyama's Sendai 2nd Division, minus the shattered 4th Regiment; a total of perhaps 16,000 men. The division's motto was: "Remember that death is lighter than a feather, but that duty is heavier than a mountain." For the Sendai, feathers flew in great numbers; the mountain proved too heavy. They were held off by a determined battalion of Marines under "Chesty" Puller, with the help of an Army battalion under Lieutenant Colonel Robert Hall. It was possible the patrol Paige had wounded, having missed its way in the darkness, was really part of that other fight. More likely, however, it was the point patrol for a battalion or possibly even a regiment, whose target was to be Colonel Hanneken's battalion.

The force was, in fact, a composite of survivors of previous battles. Under Colonel Akinosuke Oka, it included the remnants of the Ichiki Detachment and the Kawaguchi Brigade, men who had been beaten, not to say humiliated, and who could therefore be expected to fight all the harder to restore their sagging self-esteem.

49

Oka was supposed to have attacked in concert with Maruyama's division, but he had been held back by the jungle, and was one day late.

Paige and his men were not storybook Marines. They would cheerfully have done without a battle. But they were quietly confident they could acquit themselves with honor if the occasion arose. They considered themselves, without exception, the best machine gunners in the entire Corps. They were in top physical and mental condition, despite a general prevalence of malaria. They'd trained together as a unit for almost two years in the Carolinas, in Cuba, and in British Samoa. They had, furthermore, applied themselves to improving their firepower by using an idea originally conceived by Captain Michael M. Mahoney while on China duty in the 1930's.

Mahoney, a former company commander of Paige's, and Sergeant William Agee (both subsequently killed on Guadalcanal) had worked on machine gun bolts in the following manner: holes drilled in the bolts to lighten them, thus increasing recoil, and double springs used in the back plates, together with a stronger driving spring. The result was a rate of fire of about 1,300 rounds per minute. All the guns in Paige's platoon had been altered in this way.

The effectiveness of these technical innovations had been proved weeks earlier when, after a dogfight with some Grumman Wildcats, a Zero came down to strafe Paige's camp area. Paige jumped to a gun and fired back. The Zero took several hits, then crashed into a ridge line about a mile away. Two days later a Marine named Willingham shot down another Zero in the same manner. This was very good shooting indeed.

When darkness fell on October 25, they were subdued; but as far as Paige could tell, determined to hold the ridge which they had been asked to defend "at any cost."

"The Japs are definitely coming," Paige told his men. "We'll have a hundred percent watch. Don't fire until you actually see something."

During the early hours of the night there were no enemy troops to be seen, but a hearty exchange of artillery shells between 7 and 8 P.M. clearly presaged an attack. Most of the enemy shells landed behind the ridge, east of the battalion command post and in the mortar platoon area. Just before midnight, probing patrols reported a large enemy force moving toward Fox Company's positions. These were Colonel Oka's men, in strength somewhat less than a regiment.

During the day, Paige had had a good opportunity to inspect his position. To the front, the ridge sloped gently down towards a draw, covered over by six foot high *kunai* grass through which the enemy could crawl undetected. Beyond the draw, about 60 or 70 yards distant, the jungle began. To Paige's left, between him and Fox Company, was a heavily overgrown gully. There, the steep cliffsides, some 70 feet high, would make difficult climbing for an attacking force, but the tangled foliage would provide excellent concealment to the very base of the ridge. It was not altogether an ideal defensive position. For one thing, the intervening presence of supporting riflemen would prevent Paige from backing up Fox Company with all but the most forwardly-emplaced of his guns. For another, the irregularity of the terrain nullified the possibility of grazing fire, greatly reducing the efficiency of the guns.

51

Paige could have provided excellent enfilading fire, from the flank, were George Company to his right to be assaulted; but as it happened, the Japanese didn't go there.

At about 2 A.M., in a silence so pervasive that men many yards apart could hear each other breathing, Paige began to sense movement all along the front and deep in the jungle to his left. He could hear the muffled clanking of equipment and, periodically, voices hissing in Japanese. These were, apparently, squad leaders giving instructions. At the same time, small colored lights began flicking on and off throughout the jungle.

"Fireflies," one man whispered. "They're coming at us with fireflies."

"Keep quiet," Paige said. "Glue your ears to the ground." He knew very well the lights were assembly signals for the enemy squads. He left his foxhole and hurriedly gave his gun crews some last minute instructions.

"Don't fire your guns," he said. "Muzzle flash'll give away our position and we'll be smothered with grenades. I'll give the word when to fire. When things start popping, just hang on."

Paige requested an artillery and mortar concentration. This was, however, denied, because the enemy was still in the jungle where the effect would be almost nil. He returned to his foxhole near the forward lip of the knoll to await developments. Manning the number two gun, to his left, were Corporal Raymond Gaston and Private Samuel Leiphart. Their gun was set up very near where the jungle came up to meet the ridge. They reported hearing considerable rustling in the bushes.

"Hold your fire," Paige whispered.

In a foxhole nearby, Corporal Richard Stansberry arranged several grenades in a neat row in front of him. Then nervously he rearranged them.

Everybody was straining to hear and to see. The bushes rustled and the maddening voices continued their soft, sibilant mutterings, but still nothing could be seen. Then Paige dimly sensed a dark figure lurking near Gaston's position. He grabbed a grenade, pulling the pin but holding the spoon down. Behind him, he could hear the clicking as the others did the same. Somebody shrieked and instantaneously the battle erupted. Grenades began exploding on the ridge nose. Japanese rifles and machine guns fired blindly in the night and the first wave of enemy troops swarmed into the Marine positions from the jungle flanking Gaston's gun.

Stansberry was pulling the pins out of his grenades with his teeth and rolling them downslope; Leiphart was skying them overhand like a baseball pitcher. The tension burst like a balloon and many men found themselves cursing, growling, screaming like banshees. The Japanese were yelling *banzai*, and "Blood for the Emperor"; Stansberry, in a spontaneous tribute to President Roosevelt's wife, shouted back, "Blood for Eleanor!"

The battleground was lit by flashes of machine gun fire, pierced by the arching red patterns of tracer bullets, shaken by the blast of shells laid down no more than 30 yards in front of the ridge by Captain Louis Ditta's 60-mm. mortars. It was a confusing maelstrom, with dark shapes crawling across the ground or swirling in clumped knots; struggling men falling on each other with bayonets, swords and violent oaths. After the first volley of American grenades exploded, the wave of Japanese crowding onto the knoll thickened.

"Fire," Paige shouted, "Machine guns, fire!"

Paige's guns opened up and with them the supporting rifles. In the flickering light, Paige saw a fierce struggle taking place for the number two gun. Several Japanese soldiers were racing towards Leiphart, who was kneeling, apparently already hit. Paige shot two of them while the third lowered his bayonet and lunged. Leiphart was the smallest man in the platoon, weighing barely 125 pounds. The Japanese soldier ran him through, the force of the thrust lifting him high in the air. Paige took careful aim and killed Leiphart's killer. Gaston was flat on his back, scrambling away from a Japanese officer who was hacking at him with a two-handed Samurai sword and grunting with the exertion. Gaston tried desperately to block the Samurai sword with his rifle. One of his legs was already nearly severed from the blows. The rifle soon splintered. The Japanese officer raised his sword for the killing thrust and Gaston, with maniac strength, snaked his good leg up and caught his man under the chin with the boot, a violent blow that broke his neck.

The attackers ran past Gaston's gun and spread out, concentrating their fire on the left flank gun, manned by Corporal George Grant, Pfcs Sam H. Scott and Willis A. Hinson. Within minutes, Scott was killed and Hinson was wounded in the head. Stansberry, next to Paige, had been hit in the shoulder, but he was still firing his tommy gun with ferocity and shouting, "Charge, charge, blood for Eleanor!"

Corporal Pettyjohn, on the right, cried out in anguish, "My gun's jammed!"

Paige was too busy to answer his call for help. At the center forward gun, he was beating back the seemingly endless wall of Japanese coming up the gentle slope at the front of the position. There were, at that point, approximately 75 enemy soldiers crashing through the platoon, most of them on the left flank, but the main force of the attack had already begun to ebb. They started to melt back down the slope, and almost before they were out of sight, Navy corpsmen began snaking forward to treat the wounded. At the center gun, James McNabb and Mitchel F. Swanek were badly hurt and had to be moved off the line. Stansberry, not so badly hurt, refused to go. Paige crawled over to Pettyjohn's gun.

"What's wrong with it?"

"Ruptured cartridge," Pettyjohn said.

"Move over." Paige fumbled with stiff fingers, broke a nail, pried the slug out and changed the belt feed pawl while Pettyjohn and Pfc Wilson Faust covered him. Though the first assault had flopped, a number of enemy soldiers had shinnied to the top of the tall hardwood trees growing up from the jungle between the platoon and Fox Company. From this vantage point they could direct a punishing, plunging fire down in two directions. The men in foxholes along the crest were especially vulnerable; among them, Pawlowski was killed by this fire and Bob G. Jonjeck and John W. Price wounded, and helped back to an aid station by corpsmen.

Paige, getting ready to feed a new ammo belt into Pettyjohn's gun, felt a sharp vibration and a jab of hot pain on his hand. He fell back flapping his arm and staring angrily at the gun, which had been wrecked by a burst of fire from a Japanese Nambu light machine gun.

Almost immediately, a second assault wave came

washing over the Marine positions. This attack was more successful than the first. In the Fox Company area, across the gully, the Japanese swarmed up the 70-foot cliff in great numbers, armed with three heavy and six light machine guns, a number of tommy guns and several knee mortars. At 4:20, Fox had been reinforced by Captain A. Rea and 24 men from battalion headquarters, but the momentum of the Japanese charge carried the ridge, driving the Marines back and capturing three .30-calibre light machine guns. By 5 A.M., the enemy held the spur, and were threatening to overrun Paige's left flank and roll up the entire battalion front. A second prong of the attack, aimed at Paige's front, had not fared as well, but Paige's platoon was being decimated. A hail of shrapnel killed Daniel R. Cashman, leaving Paige to fire the forward gun unaided. Shortly afterwards, Stansberry's strength gave out and he was dragged back to safety by Navy corpsmen. At Pettyjohn's gun, Pfc Charles H. Lock was killed. At the left flank gun, Hinkley and Dudley were hit; Hinson, already wounded, continued to fire until all his supporting rifles were silenced. He then withdrew to higher ground in the direction of George Company, putting the gun out of action before he left, as Paige had instructed.

At the forward gun, Paige continued to trigger bursts until the barrel began to steam. In front of him was a large pile of dead bodies. He left his overheated gun when he could no longer fire it safely and ran through a flaring canopy of bullets from gun to gun to help keep them firing. At each emplacement he found only dead bodies. He knew then, for the first time, that he was entirely on his own against the enemy. He was too concerned to keep the guns firing to panic at this discovery. His only conscious thought was that "it was lonely up there with nothing but dead slopeheads for company." Running from gun to gun, he often bumped into enemy soldiers who were, seemingly, dashing aimlessly about. Apparently, they weren't yet aware they had almost complete possession of the knoll.

Paige stumbled over to his right flank and into the George Company area. There he found a couple of Marines from How Company named Kelly and Totman manning their machine gun.

"I need a gun," Paige gasped, "Follow me back." They did as they were told, without question, and while he was about it, Paige also borrowed some George Company riflemen to form a skirmish line. It was by then not quite so dark as it had been. Soon dawn would break. Paige knew that once the Japanese realized how much progress they'd made, still a third wave of attackers would come up the slope to solidify their hold on the knoll. He ordered all the Marines in the area to fix their bayonets, then led them into the fight.

On the way back, they came across a large number of Japanese soldiers advancing from Fox Company's spur back over the crest of the ridge towards Major Conoley's command post. Paige fired nearly a full belt of ammunition, about 250 rounds, into their midst, killing some and sending the rest flying back to the spur. The impromptu skirmish line started firing into the center of Paige's knoll, which was now swarming with enemy troops. After Kelly and Totman set up their machine gun and joined in, the fire began to take effect. The Japanese fell back. Several of them, however, began crabbing awkwardly across the knoll with their rifles cradled in the crooks of their arms, and Paige saw with horror that they were heading towards one of his guns, out in the open and long since unmanned.

Galvanized by the threat, Paige ran for the gun. From across the gully, several Japanese machine guns spotted him and swiveled to rake him with enfilading fire. The snipers in the trees also tried to bring him down, and grenades and mortars burst all about him as he ran to the gun. One of the crawling enemy soldiers saw him, jumped up and raced him for the prize. Paige got to it first, hurling himself the last few feet into the foxhole. The enemy soldier, less than 25 yards way, dropped to the ground and opened up on the Marine. Paige turned the machine gun on him and discovered to his shock that it was empty. He scooped up a partially loaded belt of ammo lying alongside the gun and with fumbling fingers inserted it. After what seemed an eternity, with bullets whining about his head, he got the gun working. He sprayed the terrain, clearing it of the last of the enemy troops.

All the Japanese fire at this point was being aimed at Paige, as his was the only automatic weapon firing from a forward position. The barrage, concentrated on the ridge nose, made him feel as if "the whole Japanese army" was firing at him. A Nambu machine gun seemed for an awful moment to zero in on him. The bullets whizzed by so close to his head that his ears began to ring; but luckily the fire faded off to his left.

Paige was getting some help from the mortars, controlled by battalion with George Company commander Captain L.W. Martin observing. These rounds, laid on the captured spur, prevented an enemy move forward which would have enveloped Paige from the rear. Other than this, he was alone.

In addition to manning a very dangerous, highly exposed position under heavy fire, Paige also had another worry: ammunition. He was running low, and wondering where he'd get more, when aid came in a form that made him glow with pride. Three men of his platoon voluntarily crossed the field of fire to resupply him. First a Marine named Stat ran up with a full belt. He had no sooner arrived and jumped into the foxhole than he fell with a bullet in his stomach. Dashing through the rain of bullets with another belt, a Pfc Reilly got as far as the lip of the emplacement, only to be wounded in the groin. Knocked off his feet by the round, he fell against Paige, knocking him away from the gun. Seconds later, a boy named Jonjeck, who had already been wounded once and come back on line, came charging up with a third belt of ammo. He also was hit. Turning to receive the ammunition, Paige saw a piece of flesh fly off Jonjeck's neck.

Paige told him to go back for medical aid. Jonjeck refused.

"Get the hell back," Paige shouted.

"No, I'm staying with you," the wounded Marine insisted.

Paige punched him on the chin, hard enough to bowl him over and, convinced finally that Paige wanted his orders obeyed, Jonjeck made his way safely back to the battalion C.P.

While Paige was singlehandedly holding off the enemy on the knoll, Major Conoley, at the C.P., was rounding up a ragtag force with which to retake the Fox Company spur. They were bandsmen serving as litterbearers, wiremen, runners, cooks, even mess boys who had brought some hot food up to the front lines during the night and stayed "just in case." These men, numbering no more than 24, mounted a counterattack that drove the enemy back into the jungle, recapturing the three lost light machine guns plus almost all the Japanese hardware, which was abandoned in the face of the determined Marine counterthrust. The enemy also left 98 dead on the spur, by actual count.

That was at 5:30 A.M.; dawn was already breaking. Paige was able to observe the progress of the charge from his foxhole, and was witness to the large numbers of enemy soldiers scrambling off the spur into the jungle below. Watching them, Paige was so worked up, so swept along by the excitement of the counterattack, that he decided to join them.

On China duty, he had picked up a few words of Japanese, and now decided they might come in handy. He turned his gun downslope towards the waist-high *kunai* grass and shouted, "*Tate! Tate! Tate! Isogu!* Stand up! Stand up! Stand up! Hurry!"

Immediately, a large group of Japanese, about thirty men, popped into view. One of them looked quizzically in his direction through field glasses. Paige triggered a long burst, and "they peeled off like grass under a mowing machine." At that point, Paige was so wound up he couldn't stop. He ran back to the George Company riflemen he had borrowed and told them he meant to charge off the knoll. "And I want you to be right behind me," he said. He draped two full belts of ammo around his shoulders, unclamped the heavy machine gun and cradled it in his arms. He was hardly aware of the weight, which was more than 80 pounds; and no more aware that the water jacket of the gun, it having been fired so continuously, was red-hot.

He fed one of the belts into the gun and started forward, down the slope, scrambling to keep his footing, spraying a raking fire all about him. There were still a number of live enemy soldiers on the hillside, pressed against the slope. Paige, taking them utterly by surprise, cut them all down. One of them, he noticed, was a field grade officer, no more than four feet from the machine gun when he fell dead.

The skirmishers followed Paige over the rim of the knoll and, like him, they were stirred and fired-up; shrieking and cat-calling like young boys imitating Marines. They followed Paige all the way across the draw to the edge of the jungle where, long hours before, the Japanese attacks had started. There they found nothing left to shoot at. The battle was over. The jungle was once again so still that, if it weren't for the evidence of dead bodies, the agony and torment of the previous hours, the bursting terror of the artillery shells and the thousands of rounds of ammunition that were fired might only have been a bad dream of awful death. It was always that way after a battle. "A strange sort of quietness," Paige called it.

Feeling suddenly very weary, Paige sat down. He was soaked in perspiration. Steam rose in clouds from his gun.

Captain Ditta, who had joined the riflemen in the skirmish line, came up to Paige and slapped him on the back. "Tremendous," he crowed. "Tremendous." Ditta offered Paige his canteen. Paige drank the tepid water gratefully.

Only then did he notice a painful sensation in his hand. He rolled up his tattered shirt sleeve and saw a long, angry blister running from his fingertips all the way up his forearm. Ditta also discovered a wound. He had a bullet hole in his leg.

"I guess we both better get to an aid station," Ditta grinned.

A battalion count of the draws and ravines in the sector placed the number of enemy dead at 200, most of them having fallen trying to wrest the knoll from Paige. The unpleasant chore of disposing of these bodies was accomplished in some cases by dragging them into the jungle and out of the sunlight and, in others, by burying them in shell craters; but there were very many of them, and it finally became necessary to dynamite-blast a portion of the knoll to cover them—thus eliminating a good part of the real estate for which the battle had been fought.

Three days later, Colonel Hanneken's weary battalion marched the ten miles back to Henderson Field, not for a rest, but to fight advance elements of the Nagoya 38th Division, General Hyakutate's last resource. Guadalcanal was by no means yet won, though the destruction of the Ichiki Detachment, the Kawaguchi Brigade and the Sendai 2nd Division seemed to presage victory. Control of operations passed to Army hands on December 9, and by the end of that month, the 1st, 5th and 7th Marine Regiments departed for Australia. The fighting continued until the first week in February, when Japanese destroyers evacuated some 11,000 survivors of Hyakutate's 17th Army. Control of Guadalcanal passed finally and irrevocably into American hands.

Paige was the second Marine enlisted man of the war to win a Medal of Honor, the first, Sergeant John "Manilla John" Basilone, having won his one night earlier in the stand south of Henderson by Colonel Puller's battalion. Paige subsequently was commissioned in the field and rose to the rank of colonel, but he always felt a special bond with the men who fought alongside him the night the fireflies attacked.

"No man," he insisted, "could beat that gang."

Lieutenant Commander Bruce McCandless receiving his Congressional Medal of Honor from Admiral Ernest King aboard U.S.S. *San Francisco*

3
BLACK FRIDAY
THE THIRTEENTH

LIEUTENANT COMMANDER
BRUCE McCANDLESS
U.S.S. San Francisco
NOVEMBER 13, 1942

THE BATTLE for Guadalcanal could not have been won without a supply line able to maintain a flow of grenades and guns, rations and reinforcements and medical supplies, fuel, and all the other necessities of an army in the field. Consequently much thought and effort on the part of Vice Admiral William Halsey's Noumea headquarters went into battering the Japanese life line; at Truk, Vice Admiral Isoroku Yamamoto entertained similar evil designs on American transport shipping. Yamamoto's Combined Fleet, though superior numerically, and effectively in control of the waters around Guadalcanal, rarely ventured down the Slot during daylight hours, owing to the Henderson-based air power, which the enemy rightly feared. As a result, a peculiar

65

pattern of control developed, in which the U.S. held sway from first light to dusk, and the Japanese, well trained to nighttime main battery and torpedo fire, ruled the waves from sunset to dawn. In darkness, the Tokyo Express arrived almost nightly to land reinforcements and supplies and to discharge shells on Marine positions. At such times as the small American fleet felt strong enough to challenge the forays, a night action resulted.

The names of these punishing engagements evoke the memory of one of the bitterest phases of the Pacific struggle: the Battle of Savo Island; of the Eastern Solomons; of Cape Esperance; the Battle of the Santa Cruz Islands; the Naval Battle of Guadalcanal; the Battle of Tassafaronga. So many ships, indeed, were sunk during these epic encounters that the troubled waters between Guadalcanal, Savo and Florida Islands came to be known as "Ironbottom Bay." Squadrons of battered hulks lie at rest in this graveyard of ships of war, where thousands of men lost their lives to shell and shark. One survivor recalled it as a "tour of duty in Green Hell."

On October 14, 1942, Japanese battleships *Kongo* and *Haruna* steamed unmolested to within a mile offshore Guadalcanal and pasted the airfield with 1,000 incendiary and fragmentation shells. This bruising bombardment set off fires that burned through the night and well into the following day. Japanese soldiers were ecstatic. Captain Tameichi Hara of the Imperial Japanese Navy reported that they were "thrilled and encouraged by this spectacle, and urged the Navy to repeat the show." The damage was so great that American Marines thereafter referred to the battleship strike as "The Bombardment." But it was by no means the last.

As usual, the increase in ship-to-shore shelling was accompanied by the landing of troops, which signified one of the periodic Japanese attempts to overwhelm the Marine garrison. The battle which took place on October 24–26 is described in the preceeding chapter. The dismal results, followed one day later by the Battle of the Santa Cruz Islands (in which the U.S. lost the aircraft carrier *Hornet*), left the Japanese not one whit closer to capture of Guadalcanal; if anything, prospects seemed a bit brighter for America.

A regiment of the Nagoya 38th Division landed east of Henderson Field near Koli Point on November 2. Within eight days, 850 of them (more than half) had been killed by Colonel Herman Hanneken's Battalion, and by Carlson's Raiders in a guerrilla snipe as the beaten regiment retreated through the jungle. Nevertheless, during this period, the main body of the Nagoya 38th did land safely at Tassafaronga and Kukumbona, west of the Matanikau River. To equalize this threat, Rear Admiral Richmond K. Turner, Commander, Amphibious Forces South Pacific, dispatched three attack cargo ships and four transports carrying some 6,000 Army and Marine troops to Guadalcanal from Espiritu Santo and Noumea. Escorting them were a support group commanded by Rear Admiral Norman Scott and another commanded by Rear Admiral Daniel J. Callaghan.

Yamamoto responded by ordering a task force south from Truk to bombard Henderson and to sink the American transports; following which, 11 troop-laden *Marus* were to disgorge a large volume of men and supplies on November 14. Neither side, as can be seen, lacked accurate intelligence; Halsey immediately countered by committing Task Force 16 (carrier *Enterprise,* battleships *South Dakota* and *Washington,* plus screening ships) to the impending clash—thereby setting the stage for the most crucial and pivotal of the Guadalcanal sea battles.

Turner's transports arrived early on November 12; by midafternoon, with the unloading still in progress, Japanese bombers appeared to challenge the operation. Only one of these planes accomplished anything. In a suicide crash aboard Admiral Callaghan's flagship cruiser *San Francisco,* the twin-engine Betty wrecked the after main battery director, the after fire control station, and the secondary conning station, known as Battle II. Some 45 men were killed or wounded, including the cruiser's Executive Officer, Commander Mark Crouter, who was badly burned.

At the same time, a Japanese raiding group under Vice Admiral Hiroaki Abe, consisting of battleships *Hiei* and *Kirishima,* light cruiser *Nagara,* and 11 destroyers, lay approximately 240 miles north of Guadalcanal, steaming south at 18 knots. Abe, a cautious man, was troubled by the possibility of surprise attack from U.S. submarines or planes. He ordered his pickets into a tight double ring formation to protect his battleships. The move was completed by 4 P.M.

Abe's raiders had not gone undetected. The sighting, by a B-17, was relayed to Admiral Turner; and, as the transports had already unloaded some ninety percent of their cargo, Turner immediately sent them back to the safety of Espiritu Santo. The warships of Admiral Callaghan's group (including in their number Admiral Scott's ships) escorted the transports eastward through

Lengo Channel, then reversed course and sped back into Ironbottom Bay. The time was then 10 P.M.

Abe had, earlier in the evening, passed into a tropical rain squall that darkened the skies, reducing visibility to near zero. The various skippers were unnerved at having to run at 18 knots in a complex formation under those conditions, but Abe was jubilant. The tropical storm, moving at the same speed and on the same bearing as the task force, was, said Abe, "a blessed squall." It protected him from American submarines. A scout plane reported sighting U.S. warships off Lunga Roads, but Abe's buoyant mood was not dashed. He expected not to have to "do business with them." At midnight, he ordered his ships into an S-turn that took them out from under the drenching rain, and 40 minutes later, they passed between Savo and Guadalcanal, heading east. The formation had become disordered. There were three columns in disarray, most of the destroyers having lost their stations. Abe made no attempt to tidy up his lines.

Callaghan's force passed Lunga Point heading westward towards Abe, having somehow gone undetected by Japanese shore observers. The single attenuated column —disposition Battle One—had four van destroyers (*Cushing, Laffey, Sterett* and *O'Bannon*) followed by cruisers *Atlanta, San Francisco, Portland, Helena* and *Juneau* and, bringing up the rear, destroyers *Aaron Ward, Barton, Monssen* and *Fletcher*. In all, 13 ships.

Helena was equipped with an improved surface-search (SG) radar. At 1:24 A.M. on November 13, she picked up three groups of ships at ranges of 27,000 to 32,000 yards. Via the Talk Between Ships (TBS) voice radio, Captain Gilbert Hoover notified the Flag.

At 1:30, Japanese observers on Guadalcanal reported no enemy men-of-war in sight. Abe sighed with relief and prepared to carry out his shore bombardment mission. The main batteries of the 29,000-ton battleships were loaded with Type-3 shells, each weighing 1,400 pounds, each crammed with hundreds of incendiary components. The magazines were stacked high with these shells, which were extremely effective against parked airplanes, buildings, and men in the open, but not half as effective against warships as armor-piercing shells. Abe had plenty of those also, but they were at the bottom of the pile and not readily accessible. The Americans apparently had left the field, however, so this fact didn't disturb the admiral. He was happily looking forward to a feast of destructions. Earlier, he had felt misgivings, but now he was content.

"It was a clear, dark night," recalled Commander Rae E. Arison, *San Francisco*'s navigator. "Not a light was showing, neither at sea nor ashore." The sea was smooth. A gentle, southeasterly breeze carried the heady fragrance of tropical flowers to men standing tensely at general quarters. More in keeping with their mood were the jagged flashes of lightning over the mountains of Guadalcanal and Florida.

In *San Francisco*'s pilot house, on the Navigating Bridge, were Captain Cassin Young, Arison, and an assortment of officers, talkers, quartermasters and helmsmen; thirteen in number. On the flag bridge, one deck below, were Admiral Callaghan and his staff of four lieutenant commanders. The badly wounded Executive, Commander Crouter, was in his cabin, swathed in bandages, being tended by a mess attendant. Crouter would have been transferred, along with the other wounded, to the transport *President Jackson*, but for his insistence that he could be of help to his successor, Commander Joe Hubbard. Hubbard was stationed aft in Battle II, which had been somewhat restored since the bomber crash the previous afternoon.

All of these officers ranked the Officer of the Deck, thirty-one-year-old Lieutenant Commander Bruce McCandless, who was the ship's communications officer. Due to the presence of communications men among Callaghan's staff, McCandless' normal duties had been rendered superfluous; and, since Arison, having acquired the additional duties of Staff Operations Officer and Task Group Pilot, was too busy to handle the navigator's function of conning (ordering the movements of) the cruiser, McCandless had volunteered for the job. He had, fortunately, attended a final briefing with the admiral that afternoon, for he was to find himself, within fifteen minutes of the start of the battle, the senior surviving officer able to conn *San Francisco*; theoretically (though not, as it turned out, actually) ordering the movements of a task group of 13 ships in the midst of one of the most disordered and violent battles in U.S. naval history.

McCandless was by no means unprepared for the crisis. He had been through the Battle of Cape Esperance a month earlier as Officer of the Deck and considered himself fairly well seasoned. Short in stature, unsmiling, slightly stiff in manner, his close-cropped curly hair and cherubic features belied his age and experience. He was a serious, conscientious professional naval officer who had, to the extent possible, been trained—and had trained himself—to, in his words, "take care of any such situation." Yet, surely, few junior officers have ever been called upon so abruptly and irrevocably, as McCandless was, to shrug off wounds, flinch doubts, and rise to the challenge of initiative and spontaneous leadership when a $30,000,000 cruiser and the lives of more than a thousand men were his to save or lose.

A graduate of the Naval Academy, class of '32, McCandless was the son of Commodore Byron McCandless, U.S.N., and therefore no stranger to the traditions of the sea. He was born in Washington, D.C., on August 12, 1911, attended schools in Annapolis and, inevitably, gravitated towards a career in the Navy. After graduation, McCandless served aboard cruisers *Louisville* and *Indianapolis* and destroyer *Case*. Following a course in General Line at Annapolis, he reported to *San Francisco* in September, 1939, and was aboard her when war broke out. The cruiser was in Pearl Harbor the morning of December 7, 1941, undergoing a routine overhaul, but was by the greatest good fortune untouched by the Japanese bombs, spared to earn 17 battle stars, receive credit for more hits on enemy vessels than any other ship in the Pacific—and engage a pair of battleships in the early hours of November 13, 1942, a Friday, with 13 ships in the American force and 13 officers and men in the cruiser's pilot house; circumstances suggesting to the superstitious that the battle would be fought under the auspices of a dark and foreboding power.

At just about the same time that Admiral Abe was loading shore bombardment ammunition into his 14-inch guns, McCandless was following Captain Young and Commander Arison up from the armored conning tower on the Signal (Flag) Bridge to the Navigating Bridge one deck higher, where there was no armor. There, in the pilot house, McCandless took the conn and Arison went aft into the chart house. At 1:40, Admiral Callaghan ordered a turn to due north. A moment later, while still executing the maneuver, the van destroyer *Cushing* sent by TBS, "There is a ship crossing bow from port to starboard, range 4,000 yards maximum." Immediately, the radio circuit was flooded with instructions and requests for information. *Cushing*, heading for a collision with the Japanese destroyer *Yudachi*, veered to port. Following her, cruiser *Atlanta* had to swing hard left to avoid a pileup. "*Atlanta*, what are you doing?" asked Callaghan. "Avoiding our own destroyers," *Atlanta* replied. "You are throwing the whole column in disorder," Callaghan complained.

At that same moment, *Yudachi* spotted the American column and promptly notified Abe. For the first time, the admiral realized he had a fight on his hands. Horrified —he was "visibly shaken" reported Captain Hara—he shouted for the *Hiei* and *Kirishima* gunners to dig deep into the magazines for armor-piercing shells. There was panic and bedlam as the sailors struggled to load the AP shells and to clear the decks on which, for some reason, incendiary shells had been stacked. They expected to be fired on momentarily, and one hit on the decks could threaten to blow up the entire battleship. But, inexplicably, the Americans didn't fire.

The Battle One column had gone all to pieces by then. Callaghan wanted all ships to maintain course north. Some ships heard the orders and rang up the changes, but others steered 45 degrees left of north and others due west. *Atlanta* was still turning hard left. The two forces began to interweave. *Cushing*, *Sterett*, *Laffey* and *O'Bannon* crossed astern of *Yudachi* and *Harusame*, which disappeared off to starboard. *Atlanta* closed the high, looming silhouettes of *Nagara* and *Hiei*. The TBS was a welter of confusing requests and demands:

"What do you make of it now?"

"We have a total of ten targets."

"*Fletcher*, have you come around yet?"

"Torpedoes passing from port to starboard."

"I have come 25 degrees to left."

"Range 2,246 yards."

And, from Commander Stokes in *Cushing*, repeatedly, "Shall I let them have a couple of fish?"

At 1:45 Stokes' request was granted, but too late. Both *Yudachi* and *Harusame* were by then out of range.

At 1:48, Callaghan finally gave up trying to shape up his line and ordered, "Commence firing, odd-numbered ships to starboard, even-numbered ships to port." This turned out to be an unfortunate order, as some odd-numbered ships found no targets to starboard, and some even-numbered ships found no targets to port. Several of the smaller ships found targets, however. *Cushing* and *Sterett* opened up on a destroyer to starboard, probably *Yukikaze*; and cruiser *Juneau* fired on *Yudachi*. On several Japanese ships, searchlight shutters, clicked open and the beams blinked across the waters, pinpointing *Atlanta*, which promptly veered across *San Francisco's* bow. With the threat of a collision imminent, McCandless called down the voice tube to the Flag Bridge, "*Atlanta's* turning left. Shall I follow her?" Advised to hold

74

his course, he watched the gap narrowing; then, a few seconds later, the order, "Follow the *Atlanta!*" came not a moment too soon. McCandless swung right to clear, then used full left rudder.

San Francisco pulled parallel to *Atlanta* just as a salvo of shells crashed into the other cruiser's superstructure, and one of these rounds killed Admiral Scott. Wounded *Atlanta* lurched northward to be staggered further by two torpedoes from *Akatsuki*.

Further back in the column, the Japanese destroyer *Yudachi*, having crossed the American formation heading northeast, turned 360 degrees and came knifing through the line between *Juneau* and *Aaron Ward*. Moving southeast behind *Yudachi*, *Amatsukaze* fired off eight torpedoes. *Aaron Ward* veered sharply to avoid a collision with *Yudachi*. Behind her, destroyer *Barton* stopped abruptly to avoid hitting *Aaron Ward*, and at that moment, two of *Amatsukaze's* torpedoes struck—one in the forward fire room and one in the forward engine room. Broken in two, *Barton* went down with ninety percent loss of life.

Simultaneously, Callaghan discovered that some of *San Francisco's* shells were pumping into crippled *Atlanta*, and ordered, "Cease firing own ships."

A babble of incredulous voices flooded the TBS. Cruiser *Portland's* skipper asked, "What's the dope? Did you want to cease fire?" Callaghan replied, "Affirmative." The time was then 1:53 and the preliminary skirmishes hadn't yet erupted into a full-scale engagement. The two Japanese battleships were just then steaming into view. Ignoring Callaghan's order, *Cushing*, already hit amidships and with her power lines out; *Sterett*, hit and with steering and radar out; and *Laffey*, passing so close to the giant *Hiei* that she was almost cut in two by the towering prow, began to tangle with the behemoth. The puny destroyers, like gnats assaulting an elephant, closed in and loosed torpedoes. *Cushing*'s missed. *Laffey* was so close her fish failed to arm. *Sterett*'s missed. *Laffey* raked *Hiei*'s superstructure with 20-mm. and 1.1-inch fire, killing Captain Suzuki and wounding Admiral Abe and a number of others. *Hiei* struck back with a furious salvo from her heavy guns and destroyer *Terutsuki* planted a torpedo in *Laffey*'s stern. The destroyer went down instantly with heavy loss of life. *Cushing*, mortally wounded, drifted for a while, then came to a dead stop in the water. *Sterett*, radar shot away and steering gear mauled, escaped further damage and retired through the Japanese destroyer screen.

Callaghan saw the courageous midgets challenge the *Kongo*-class battleship and nodded approvingly. "We want the big ones," he broadcast. "Get the big ones first." It was to be his last order.

O'Bannon came to within 1,200 yards of *Hiei*, fired two torpedoes, then peppered the battleship's decks with her 5-inchers. She was so close that the mighty *Hiei* couldn't depress her big guns sufficiently; the 14-inch shells coursed overhead; and so *O'Bannon* made a safe withdrawal to the southeast. On the way out, some of her crewmen noted the flames wreathing *Hiei*, partly their own handiwork, and partly due to *San Francisco*'s 8-inch guns.

While the destroyers were sniping at the battlewagon, Callaghan's flagship moved along *Hiei*'s starboard side at a range of 2,500 yards and opened fire. At the same time, some of *Hiei*'s turrets turned to bear on the cruiser. *San Francisco* fired first; seconds later, *Hiei* answered, to be joined by *Nagara*'s 5.5-inch batteries and, further back, *Kirishima*'s 14-inchers. Several destroyers also joined in. *San Francisco* took *Akatsuki* under fire, as did one or two destroyers. Seven salvos rained down on her decks. Burning from stem to stern, the Japanese destroyer retired, only to go down shortly afterwards.

Simultaneously, farther to the east, torpedoes from *Amatsukaze* broke *Juneau*'s keel, putting her out of action; destroyer *Monssen* fired torpedoes at *Kirishima*, and cruisers *Helena* and *Portland* were squaring off with several Japanese destroyers. *Barton* and *Laffey* were already sunk, burning *Atlanta* was little more than a spectator and *Fletcher*, with her paint hardly flaked, was steaming erratically through the cannonading in search of targets. It was the high point in noise and maneuver and flaring color: the yellow of guns going off, the red, white and blue of tracers, the white of star shells, the dull red of flames; *San Francisco* was circling west towards Guadalcanal as *Hiei* circled left towards Savo, wary antagonists. Abe's nerves were already frayed. He wanted no more of the confused, impossibly chaotic battle in which a commander hardly knew what half his force was about. At about 2 A.M. he ordered *Hiei* and *Kirishima* out to sea. During the following ten minutes, as the battleship fired intermittently while turning away, a salvo from *Hiei* finally found the mark on *San Francisco*.

The first shell hit starboard aft of the pilot house. Commander Arison had just gone into the chart room to look at the target plot when the shell burst, killing a radioman a foot away and shattering the navigator's right arm. He picked himself up from the deck and, meaning to report to Captain Young, had gone as far as the curtained doorway to the pilot house when a second shell landed on the starboard side, mortally wounding the captain and hurling Arison through the air.

"It blew me clear across the bridge, passing between the wheel and the engine room telegraph," Arison recalled. He hit the bridge screen and passed out cold.

McCandless had fared somewhat better. Seconds before the blasts, he had moved towards the port side of the pilot house. He was knocked off his feet and stunned by the concussion. He had a minor fragment wound—a sliver of steel imbedded in his head—but it hadn't pierced anything vital, and there was relatively little blood. McCandless staggered up and moved off and, just as he did, several more shells struck near where he'd been standing. A hailstorm of steel crosshatched the pilot house, scoring the bulkheads and cutting down nearly every man there. Clouds of acrid smoke billowed. Here and there little tongues of flame flickered. McCandless sat up shaking his head. He was dazed and there was a persistent ringing in his ears which he couldn't shake. The acrid smoke stung his eyes; as it began to dissipate, he looked around and saw only one man standing, helmsman Harry Higdon. As for the others, there was a jumble of bodies.

In Battle II, Commander Joe Hubbard, the acting Executive, was unable to raise either of the bridge stations by phone. He ordered steering and engine control shifted to him. Seconds later, his station was destroyed by a large calibre shell, and all hands in Battle II were killed. The stricken cruiser plunged through the foam at 18 knots, circling left with standard rudder. Nobody was at the helm; in the pilot house, Higdon, who had survived the avalanche of shells without a mark on him, spun his wheel helplessly. He turned to McCandless, who had gotten to his feet—the only other man standing—and said, "I've lost steering control." McCandless blanched. As far as he knew, there were seven following vessels taking their cues from *San Francisco.* (Actually, things were so fouled that each ship was on its own.)

At that moment, there was a screeching in the voice tube, from the conning tower below. "I have steering and engine control down here," the voice kept repeating. McCandless and Higdon raced down to the Signal Bridge and found Quartermaster 3/C Floyd Rogers, the secondary steersman, alone in conn. McCandless peered through the forward slits, orienting himself with the lights from shell flashes, searchlights and star shells. He made out the dim silhouette of Savo Island off the starboard bow; *San Francisco* was still circling towards Guadalcanal.

McCandless gave Rogers a course to steer, then started back up to the Navigating Bridge to see if Captain Young was able to resume command.

Two decks above the Navigating Bridge, in Main Battery Control Forward (a fire control platform, just below the radar antenna and high above the two forward turrets, which provided excellent visibility during daylight hours, but not so good for a night action) were the Gunnery Officer, Lieutenant Commander William Wilbourne, directing the 8-inch guns, and the Assistant Gunnery Officer, Lieutenant Commander James Cone, directing the 5-inch guns. Cone was using the starboard battery of 5-inch guns to fire star shells for illuminating purposes (they were mostly ineffectual against destroyers in any case) so Wilbourne could lay his 8-inch on a target and really do some damage. Trading blows with *Hiei* in this manner, they scored many hits and, shortly, the Japanese battleship began burning fiercely. From *Amatsukaze*, she was seen to be "silhouetted by her own fires."

The American cruiser also had taken a number of hits, however, and was badly battered. Fires sprang up along her deck. In the pilot house, Arison came to and found himself amid a grisly junkyard of jagged steel, surrounded by broken gear and dead bodies in limp, awful postures. Arison got to his feet slowly and painfully and lurched out of the pilot house to the port bridge wing, an open platform. Two men had lowered a line and were about to slide down four decks to the gun platform. Mc-Candless was, at that point, on his way up from the conning tower, a short distance made endless by flames, smoke and ladders torn from their moorings. After the sailors slid down the line, Arison, with one shattered arm dangling, started to follow, and just at that moment a cascade of shells struck home on the cruiser.

One or two of these, 6-inch from a secondary battery of *Hiei*, hit the overhead of the Flag Bridge on the starboard side and, bursting through, exploded in the enclosed space. Admiral Callaghan and three of his lieutenant commanders were killed instantly; the fourth, Lieutenant Commander Emmett O'Bierne, was severely wounded. Apparently the five men were standing together, with the admiral in front and the four staff officers in a row behind. All five were stacked up like logs.

At the same time, a shell landed on the port side directly below Arison who, just then hanging halfway off the open port wing above the Flag Bridge, went flying.

"The force of the explosion blew me up and over," he recalled. "I made three complete turns in the air. Below me I could see the 5-inch gun surrounded by a 1/4-inch shield. If I hit the shield I would have been cut in two. My luck held and I landed feet first on the barrel of the gun. This fractured both legs. The gun was elevated about 30 degrees so I slid down the barrel and landed in the gun captain's arms. He pushed me aside and I went through the gun shield entrance and down the ladder to the forecastle deck, below. I ended up in a corner of the deckhouse. The ship had acquired a list to starboard and everything above me was afire. Water was pouring down from above, collecting in my corner, and soon I was sitting with water up to my chest."

The water was coming from the ruptured water-cooling system of the forward 1.1-inch guns. Arriving at the Navigating Bridge, McCandless ducked through the spray and stumbled into the swirling smoke to the pilot house to search for Captain Young. He didn't have to stay very long. The chart house was a shambles; the pilot house a charnel house; nobody moved, or even cried out; it was clear to McCandless that all hands were dead or dying. He thought, "Nobody here is going to take further part in this action," and headed for the Flag Bridge to find out what orders Admiral Callaghan had for his flagship.

In all, no more than ten minutes had elapsed since the first shell struck home. The exchange of rounds between *San Francisco* and the half-dozen or so ships trying to sink her had set off a general melee involving a number of other ships. *Portland* had been hit in the stern by a torpedo from *Yudachi*; with warped plates, she was steaming helplessly in an involuntary circle. Several destroyers had tangled. *Aaron Ward* scored hits on *Yudachi*, setting her afire. *Hiei* was still burning, and now her communications went out. As she was the only ship he could recognize, Captain Hara ordered *Amatsukaze* to join the Flag. As the destroyer turned, *San Francisco* loomed up on a collision course.

"I screamed as a big ship suddenly appeared out of the darkness just in front of us," Hara wrote. Everybody cringed, the helmsman spun the wheel frantically and *Amatsukaze* veered, coming parallel at less than 200 yards from the cruiser. The two ships steamed side by side on reverse courses, the larger one in flames and blowing off huge clouds of smoke. Hara, recognizing *San Francisco*, commenced firing with his 4-inch guns.

McCandless was, at that moment, coming out of the pilot house to the port wing, which was pocked with holes and twisted into wierdly sculpted forms; he fell into a gaping crater with jagged edges that slashed his legs as he plunged down. He grasped the deck to stop his fall and, as he was trying to extricate himself, *Amatsukaze* flashed by, firing at point-blank range, hitting the bridge twice and wiping out a gun mount. Hara also fired his last four torpedoes, but they failed to arm. McCandless was, fortunately, in the after part of the bridge wing; Hara's shells landed forward. *San Fransciso* shuddered from the hits, and McCandless was thrown sliding across the slippery deck, shaken but unhurt. Through a hole in the bridge screen, he was able to see Cone's 5-inch guns answer Hara's fire. One gun, firing on local control under Chief Boatswain's Mate John McCullough, scored a hit which caused a large explosion on the destroyer's stern.

Helena also took *Amatsukaze* under fire. One of her shells landed on the bridge, knocking Hara to the deck. Another burst on the main deck, a third on the fire control platform. Altogether, 43 men were killed by the combined fire from the two American cruisers. Hara called up to ask about his fire control director, a certain Lieutenant Shimizu, and got back what must be the most bizarre reply to a reasonable question any commander ever received:

"Lieutenant Shimizu was blasted from the ship, sir, leaving behind only one of his legs."

Hara put out a smoke screen and took his wounded ship out of range and out of the fight.

At about the same time—somewhere between 2:10 and 2:20—destroyer *Monssen* steamed into a fatal joust with destroyers *Murusame* and *Asagumo*. A burst of star shells mistakenly convinced *Monssen's* skipper that she was taking hits from friendly vessels; he flicked on his fighting lights. Two searchlight beams immediately fastened on the destroyer's bridge, followed a fraction of a second later by 37 shells that left *Monssen* a burning hulk. *Cushing* also was taken under searchlights, from *Terutsuki*, and battered by that destroyer, and by *Hiei's* big guns. It was the battleship, circling away from her engagement with *San Francisco*, who finished off the destroyer. *Monssen* and *Cushing* were both abandoned at 2:20 A.M. In this same set-to, *Sterett* had all but two of her guns knocked out and was burning badly along the superstructure. She limped out of battle to the southeast, going very slowly so as not to fan the flames.

Helena had ceased firing four minutes earlier. *Atlanta*,

Juneau and *Aaron Ward*, all badly damaged, were dead in the water. The only American ships still in action were *Fletcher*, picking its way through the confusing melange of burning ships and shooting off torpedoes; *Portland*, firing its forward turrets at retreating *Hiei*; and *San Francisco*.

McCandless had by then finally pulled himself erect; he was bemused by the terrific thumping of shells and the other mindless noises of battle: a siren over the Navigating Bridge whining incessantly, flames crackling, smoke hissing, water cascading and sloshing across the decks, men shouting and cursing, tin voices nagging in the phones. A blast of flame seared his face, leaving sooty streaks. His ears were ringing and his bloody pants leg clung to his skin. Making his way down to the Signal Bridge, he hoped to find Admiral Callaghan alive, but in the doorway leading to flag plot he found the five bodies heaped together and figured them to be beyond help. McCandless' shock at seeing so many friends and shipmates dead was all the greater for realizing how much in jeopardy the ship was. On returning to the conning tower, he was told by Higdon that Commander Hubbard had been killed and that Commander Crouter, *San Francisco*'s badly burned Executive Officer, had died from a shell bursting near his cabin.

Things were very bad indeed all over the ship. The fantail was severely battered, the cutaway amidships less so, the bridge a total wreck, the quarterdeck and main deck only half visible through a pall of smoke. Gun crews and systems had been so badly mauled by *Amatsukaze*'s close-in fire that the 5-inch, 1.1-inch and 20-mm. batteries had been all but silenced. Only the main batteries continued to speak. Throughout the ship, damage control parties scuttled about with fire equipment, training their hoses, cursing and shriveling away from the intense heat. From where he stood, McCandless could make out at least ten or fifteen separate fires blazing.

Belowdecks, things were no better. Lighting systems had shorted out, the ventilation was faltering and, due to shell holes at the water line, men in the lower compartments were trying to work in water up to their armpits, their only light coming from electric hand lanterns.

Each time the ship lurched, McCandless felt a stab of apprehension. *San Francisco* was behaving strangely, due to the great amounts of water she had taken, and McCandless wasn't at all sure she could be saved. For the moment, however, she was taking no hits, and was slowly edging out of range of *Hiei*'s guns.

There was good interior communications via the sound-powered battle phones, and this very much increased the hope of restoring a semblance of order. Rogers, serving as McCandless' talker, contacted Central Station. McCandless said: "Notify Commander Schonland that he appears to be the senior surviving officer." Lieutenant Commander Herbert Schonland, whose station was Damage Control Central deep in the innards of the cruiser, had inherited the duties of the Damage Control Officer. So far as McCandless could tell, every officer senior to Schonland was either dead or out of action.

McCandless stood near a slit in the conning tower, with binoculars to his eyes. Intermittently, as the dense, oil-heavy smoke gusted, he was able to see the dull, angry glare of shellfire, curlicues of vivid star shell colors spiral-

85

ing down from flaring seminal globes like pastry tails, and on the surface of the sea, a number of ships aflame and sagging. Firing seemed pretty well to have died down throughout the sound; only an occasional gruff bark boomed.

Rogers had passed his words along, and because of a conference feature, it was heard by the Engineering Officer, Lieutenant Commander Rodney Lair, who was then far below in the after engine room. Lair immediately started up to the bridge to give McCandless a hand—the engineering plant itself was virtually unscathed—but because of the chaos and the continuing fall of shells at random moments throughout his trip, it took him such a long time that the battle had ended before he arrived; and when he did arrive, he couldn't see anything because his eyes weren't accustomed to the darkness.

Wilbourne also got the word. "If you like I'll come down to relieve you, or send Jim Cone down," Wilbourne offered.

"No," McCandless replied, "We'll never need good gunnery more than we do right now. Just keep on shooting, I'm making out fine."

Schonland finally got to the phone and told McCandless to "hang on up there." Schonland was himself coping with a job he'd inherited only hours earlier from Commander Hubbard. His Damage Control parties had to fight some twenty fires then raging throughout the ship, and to counter the flooding caused by holes at the water line. Schonland (who was also to win a Medal of Honor) was figuratively and literally inundated. He had an assistant, Ensign Dusch, but *San Francisco*'s state was so perilous that every hand—and every moment—weighed

86

heavily. "Hang on to it," Schonland told McCandless. "Just keep on doing what you're doing. We're up to our armpits down here."

San Francisco and *Hiei* were by then quite a distance apart and visible to each other only intermittently, but both continued to lash out at each other, and one of these periodic salvos from *Hiei* hurt the cruiser once again. One shell struck in the midst of a repair party headed by Ensign Vanderhoof, wiping it out entirely, and another landed on the bridge not two feet above McCandless' head. He was then peering out the slit. The shell shredded the deck of the pilot house above, tearing the steering wheel off its pedestal. Steel plates curled in like paper set to flame and the entire conning tower was peppered with fragments, some of which came in through the slits. McCandless' eyes were saved only because he had his binoculars up, but the blast flung him backwards, knocking him out cold.

He came to only short moments later, lifting his head groggily to stare at shadowed shapes that puzzled him at first. He sat up, slowly, and came unfogged. He felt himself for wounds; surprised to discover there were none, he got up unsteadily. Neither Rogers nor Higdon had been hit. Rogers reported, "We have lost steering and engine control. And the gyro repeater is out." This meant, among other things, that the cruiser no longer had a functioning compass.

(The shell hadn't actually caused the steering to go out. By sheer chance Schonland had, at just that moment, turned off all electrical circuits to the conning tower for the purpose of fighting a fire below. But McCandless couldn't know this.)

"How are the JV phones?" McCandless asked.

Part of damage suffered by the *San Francisco* during night action of November 13, 1942. View is of the Signal (Flag) Bridge.

"All right."

"Well ask Central if they have control."

Central did, and for the next few hours, McCandless passed his orders through a pair of talkers to a quartermaster in Central who actually made the steering changes as McCandless called for them. *Hiei*'s parting salvo (as it turned out to be) had caused other damage to the cruiser. A 5-inch shell demolished the after AA director, and others knocked out the ventilating system, its blowers damaged beyond repair. In the engine rooms, and in Central, heat rose precipitously. Men shucked off their khakis and worked in shorts until they fell back exhausted and half asphyxiated from the acrid fumes clogging their nostrils and searing their lungs. Both Higdon and Rogers had to take turns relieving the steersman in Central.

In the lull following *Hiei*'s last rounds, *San Francisco* steamed westward towards the channel between Savo and Guadalcanal. On the starboard beam, McCandless could see searchlights and shellfire, tracers, clusters of flaking incendiaries and star shells like inverted light bulbs; while, above the ships burning in their own fires, clouds of smoke with their undersides haloed by the flames belched skywards in gross eruptions.

Wilbourne trained his guns in that direction and, one 5-incher, on local control, popped off prematurely, setting off a brief contention; *San Francisco* came under fire, another ship went to her support, and the two dark shapes, neither one of them identifiable, began to circle each other spitting salvos. McCandless gratefully steamed past between the skirmishers. Peering out the slit a moment later, he saw a dark, looming superstructure materialize out of the gloom, and it seemed for an awful moment as though there would surely be a collision. McCandless sprang back and shouted for left full rudder. *San Francisco* turned south and at the same time, the other ship, which McCandless now recognized to be the battleship *Kirishima*, slowly began a swing northward, and began firing. Several main battery salvos fell short, the only damage, from one near miss, suffered by Number Two turret. A piece of shrapnel shorted the panel which controlled the flooding of the magazines, and the device did exactly what it was supposed to do. The lower handling room and several magazines were immersed. As *San Francisco*'s Number Three turret came around to bear, Wilbourne let fly at *Kirishima* but scored only one grazing blow with an 8-incher.

"We're in for it now," McCandless thought gloomily,

but to his great amazement, *Kirishima* continued her turn northward and sped out to sea, leaving the arena. McCandless took a deep breath.

During all this time, Rogers had periodically been reporting a request to turn on the cargo handling lights.

"Who is that from?" McCandless snapped.

Rogers shrugged his shoulders. "He won't say."

"He may have been stupid," McCandless later recalled, "but he wasn't stupid enough to tell me who or where he was."

San Francisco was then steaming towards Guadalcanal at an excessive speed, considering her condition. She was unstable due to hundreds of tons of water sloshing about on her decks. Many compartments were flooded, including sick bay, which had to be evacuated, and the cruiser was lunging and skidding drunkenly across the sound. McCandless slowed to ten knots. With no charts—all of them had been destroyed—compass, radar or fathometer, McCandless now turned to still another problem, navigation.

The night was very dark, Guadalcanal very near, and McCandless inexperienced. He had, in fact, never before navigated the ship. He was making his debut, and Rae Arison, the ship's navigator, was sitting in a corner of a deckhouse, badly wounded, with water lapping around his chest. The shock was beginning to wear off; his shattered arm hurt fiercely. He tried to reach a first aid kit attached to his belt, which contained morphine. "Every time I tried my arm hurt that much more," he recalled. "It was lucky I didn't succeed, for had I, I would have passed out and drowned in my corner. As it was, the constant fishing for the packet kept me awake."

In the absence of anything more specific to do, Mc-

Candless swung the cruiser eastward towards the American-held portion of the island, and steamed along the coast gauging the distance to the dim silhouette by eye. When it seemed to be too close he sheered off; when it vanished, he closed in. He felt very tense about this crude method, but it was the only one available to him. McCandless might have been justified in thinking it the last crisis; but, in fact, there was more to come. At 2:40 an imposing silhouette appeared out of the darkness about 2,000 yards to starboard and gradually abeam. Anxiously, McCandless peered through his binoculars and saw two stacks and five turrets. A cruiser; but whose? His doubts intensified when the turrets swung about to train on *San Francisco*.

Wilbourne called down that his turrets—except for Number Two, which was flooded and inoperative—were trained on the mystery ship, but that he was withholding fire. "I think it may be *Helena*," he said.

When the other ship flashed the letters of the American challenge, Wilbourne relaxed, but McCandless still had a serious problem. *San Francisco* recognized *Helena*, but did *Helena* recognize *San Francisco*? The challenge had been given. If there were no reply within ten seconds, *Helena* would certainly let loose with her fifteen 6-inch and four 5-inch guns. But McCandless couldn't remember the answer to the challenge.

"The carefully memorized reply had been driven from my mind by the events of the last hour," McCandless recalled. He ran to the bulkhead of the flag plot enclosure where, many hours earlier, the challenges and replies had been marked, but found only holes, dents and charred islands of paint.

There was another possible course of action: McCandless could run up one deck and turn on the three vertical fighting lights which served to identify the cruiser. But valuable seconds were ticking away, and there was always the possibility that the lights might have been damaged in the battle. Any signaling device would have served the purpose, but unfortunately, great care had been taken earlier that no flashlights or other such lights would be lying about, for fear that somebody would use them when it might endanger the ship; however, just when it seemed that the crisis would resolve itself in gunfire, a lone signalman materialized with a blinker gun under his arm.

McCandless quickly pressed him into service and had him send the message: HELENA FROM SAN FRANCISCO. ADMIRAL CALLAGHAN AND CAPTAIN YOUNG KILLED. SHIP BADLY DAMAGED. TAKE CHARGE.

Seconds later, to everybody's immense relief, *Helena*'s guns swung away.

San Francisco fell in astern of *Helena*, and some time between 3 and 4 A.M., a column of six U.S. warships (*Helena, San Francisco, Juneau, O'Bannon, Fletcher* and *Sterett*) passed through Sealark Channel heading east. At about 7:30 Lieutenant (j.g.) John Bennett, his arm in an improvised sling, relieved McCandless as Officer of the Deck; a post he had held for more than twelve hours and which he relinquished with a grateful sigh. His long ordeal was finally over. Suddenly terribly drained and weary, and sensible for the first time of his wounds, he stumbled below for treatment, a bite to eat, and a moment of relaxation.

During the retirement through Sealark Channel, the Japanese submarine *I-26* fired a spread of torpedoes at

92

San Francisco, missing by only a few feet. However, one of the torpedoes struck *Juneau*, which disappeared from view amid a huge explosion containing hundreds of smaller ones, a thunderhead spewing smoke and water in all directions. Only 14 men survived. The worst disaster of the battle, it was also the last.

When the final tabulation was taken the tactical victory was narrowly Japan's. *Hiei* (scuttled during daylight just north of Savo) and two destroyers were sunk. The U.S. lost *Juneau*, *Atlanta*, and four destroyers. Yet, in a more comprehensive view, the victory was clearly the U.S. Navy's. Henderson Field had not been shelled; its airpower was still intact. The 11 Japanese transports that were to have been landed on November 14 were attacked by this airpower and by the *Enterprise* air group and destroyed, with a loss of more than 7,000 men and most of the supplies. And on the night of the fourteenth, battleship *Washington* took on *Kirishima* and that battleship joined her sister ship *Hiei* at the bottom of Ironbottom Bay.

Despite the slight statistical edge gained in the early morning hours of November 13—Black Friday the thirteenth for many hundreds of men—Japan had failed utterly to carry out her plans. In recognition of this fact, Admiral Abe was relieved of his command.

The Naval Battle of Guadalcanal proved to be what one Japanese commentator described as "the fork in the road," a significant turning. Never again did Japan seriously threaten the American hold on the embattled island. From week to week, American strength and assurance increased. Staff planners unrolled their maps; American eyes swung northwest to Rabaul. . . .

Lieutenant Robert Hanson, left, with Captain Donald Aldrich and Captain Harold Spears

4

PATRIOTS
AND MADMEN

∞∞∞∞∞∞∞∞∞∞∞∞∞∞∞∞∞∞∞∞∞∞∞∞∞∞∞∞∞∞∞

LIEUTENANT ROBERT HANSON

Marine Fighter Squadron 215

NOVEMBER 1, 1943–FEBRUARY 3, 1944

THE AMERICAN scramble up the Solomons from Guadalcanal northwest to Bougainville in 1943 had as its final goal the strangulation of Rabaul on the northeast tip of New Britain in the Bismarcks. Rabaul was Japan's military nexus in the South Pacific, a nerve center from which naval and air forays could be raised to strike down the Slot to the southern Solomons or westward against the vulnerable flank of General Douglas MacArthur's hard-pressed army in New Guinea. Eliminating Rabaul by direct means would have required a long and costly campaign. Instead, the decision was made to mount heavy air strikes against naval and transport shipping in Rabaul's Simpson Harbor and against her military airfields—Lakunai, Rapopo, Tubera and Vunakanau dromes. Simultaneously, Marine and Army divisions were to progress up the Solomons ladder, snipping off the tentacles of Japanese power, drawing the

ring tighter around Rabaul and capturing or construct-
ing airfields as they went.

On February 21, 1943, Carlson's Raiders landed unopposed on the Russell Islands. By June there were four
bases on Guadalcanal and two more on the Russells.
During the summer, further landings were made on
Vanguna, Rendova, Kolombangara, New Georgia, Arun-
del and Vella Lavella. Some of the landings were blood-
less, others hotly contested, but by mid-October, these
islands had been won and Marine air units were making
full use of Ondonga and Munda Fields on New Georgia,
Barakoma Field on Vella Lavella, and numerous other
bases which blossomed throughout the Central Solomons like hothouse plants.

It was at Munda that Major Gregory "Pappy" Boyington and his Black Sheep—Marine Fighter Squadron
214—distinguished themselves in aerial combat and
earned headlines stateside. Boyington, with 28 kills, the
top-ranked Marine ace, was one of 11 flying Leathernecks to win the Medal of Honor, all but two of them
(Captain Henry Elrod at Wake and Captain Richard
Fleming at Midway) in the Solomons arena.

During this same period, Barakoma on Vella Lavella
was home base for VMF-215, holder of the single-tour
record of 106 Japanese planes shot down, and the first
Marine squadron to win the Navy Unit Citation. Con-
tributing to the celebrated squadron's top score were a
dazzling array of ten aces (flyers with five or more kills
to their credit), led by First Lieutenant Robert Murray
Hanson of Lucknow, India, and Newtonville,Massachu-
setts, the son of Methodist missionary parents. Hanson,
a boyish and zealous twenty-three-year-old, was a very

skillful pilot, one of the great combat flyers of World War II. His beginnings were rather modest, however, as his first tour of duty, with the Swashbuckler squadron, in August, 1943, produced only two enemy planes officially credited. Shortly, however, he would be rivaling Boyington and Captain Joe Foss for top spot in the pantheon of Marine air aces. Hanson's final score was 25 kills, and he was the only one of the top three not to survive the war.

Transferred to VMF-215 at the end of his first tour, the 200-pound, 5′ 11″ youngster, an alert, friendly, beefy man, impressed his new skipper, Major R. Gordon Owens. After watching Hanson handle his F4U Corsair in practice hops, Owens assigned him to lead a two-plane flight element, an honor rarely accorded new men. Owens evidently agreed with the appraisal of Hanson's former skipper, Major John Burnett, who had described him as "a smart youngster and a number one pilot." Hanson was so good, in fact, that several of his squadron mates, assigned to fly his wing, admitted they couldn't keep up with him.

If Hanson had a flaw, it was to be found in his seemingly irrepressible recklessness which, even for fighter pilots, was extreme. But that fault, Owens decided, could only be tempered by the harsh realities of life in a combat cockpit. Hanson would soon learn that it never paid to overreach yourself when the slightest error in judgment could send you down to the sea in flames.

On November 1, 1943, a division of four planes from VMF-215 was assigned to fly cover for the amphibious landings at Empress Augusta Bay, midway up the west coast of Bougainville Island, the last Japanese stronghold in the Solomons, and the gateway to Rabaul. The flight leader was Captain Arthur Warner. The other pilots were Lieutenants Lloyd Cox, Sam Sampler and Bob Hanson.

It was expected that the enemy would commit all available air strength to sweep the U.S. Marines off the Bougainville beaches, and in fact, Lieutenant General Haruyoshi Hyakutate, in charge of the defense, did just that. Zeroes and Zekes, Hamps, Bettys and Kates—fighters, dive bombers and torpedo bombers—rose up from landing strips throughout the island. They came from Buka in the north, Kieta on the east coast, Kahili and Ballalle and Kara in the south, and droned towards Empress Augusta Bay like so many hungry locusts. They were met by a mammoth umbrella of more than 200 Marine fighters from half a dozen squadrons, and the sky above the bay soon turned into a speckled and streaked canvas, the air filled with keening, plummeting, dying aircraft.

In the boats, Marines peered up anxiously, knowing full well that their safety was at issue. Throughout the morning, wave upon wave of Japanese planes challenged the screen of Hellcats, Wildcats and Corsairs, and below the screech and weave of the air combat, the 3rd Division, undertaking its first landing, tried mightily to ignore the struggle and go about its business, which was to consolidate the beachhead.

Shortly after noon, during a lull in the dogfighting, Captain Arthur Warner's flight of four planes from VMF-215 arrived and took its place in an assigned patrol sector, replacing a flight of Hellcats from VMF-221. Patrolling at 20,000 feet, the pilots had a panoramic view of the bay, and since for the moment there were no enemy planes in range, they were able to enjoy it. The assault waves had long since gone ashore. Most of the shipping was unloading heavy equipment, howitzers, huge cases of ammunition and supplies. The LCVP, or Higgins boat, used to carry assault troops, had given way to the larger LST, LCI, LCM and LCT—slower, more cumbersome boats, but with large carrying loads to cope with the huge amounts of matériel needed on the beaches. They were extremely vulnerable to air attack; in recognition of which fact, the troops had decided LST stood for Large Stationary Target.

Shortly after arriving, Hanson discovered that he had run out of oxygen. He tried to notify Captain Warner but his radio was on the blink. Hanson was already rather nervous, the lines in his face stiff with tension, and he had begun chain-smoking. The equipment malfunctions made him edgier still. He motioned to Warner by hand with exaggerated gestures and finally the flight leader got the message. The four Corsairs gulled down to 13,000 feet. Just as they did, Hanson caught the flash of the sun reflecting off silver wings at about 10,000 feet, and spotted a large formation of Zekes arriving from Kieta drome, perhaps 30 of them. They apparently were headed down to strafe the beaches. Hanson waved his hands wildly, caught Warner's attention, and the flight leader nodded that he had seen them. "Down we go," Warner mouthed, and broke off.

Hanson tapped out his cigarette butt and, kicking the rudder bar with his feet, pushed the stick forward. The Corsair fell off on one wing and went careening down behind Warner's.

Six of the Zekes made up a forward flight. Hanson

picked one out of this bunch, just as they broke formation to meet the attack, some continuing their dive, others nosing up to engage or circling wide for advantage. Hanson tailed in behind his target. The Japanese pilot was scorching down towards the beach when Hanson fired his first burst. The .50-calibre bullets scored the vivid Rising Sun meatball on the Zeke's right wing. The pilot seemed to be trying to pull away to the left, but he had accumulated too much speed to maneuver, and his controls were stiff and unyielding. Hanson adjusted his aim slightly and gave him a second burst. Immediately a plume of smoke burst from the Zeke. Seconds later it was in flames. Hanson pulled up as the Zeke slowed down. He passed over the burning plane and as he did, the Japanese pilot gamely elevated his nose slightly and poured out a few shells, but his aim was wide. The Zeke then fell off and down, burning as it went.

Hanson banked right, then left, his eyes darting quickly across the sky to seek out another target. His face was a frozen mask and felt like coagulating cement. Hanson was very skillful in the air, but not comfortable there, as other aces claimed to be. He fell in behind another Zeke which loomed up in his sights and instinctively pressed the firing button. Tracers arched out and hammered into the fuselage of the lightly-armored fighter. A few wisps of smoke curled back and then with frightening suddenness the plane exploded, hurling bits of metal and fabric into the air.

A pair of Zekes fell on Hanson's tail. He pulled up into a chandelle to the left and swiftly climbed 5,000 or 6,000 feet, losing them. Above the battle, he could see numerous engagements spread out over a wide area. Two

100

Japanese planes were burning and spiraling down to the sea, and so was one Corsair. Hanson wondered idly who it was, and looked about to see if he could spot Warner, Cox and Sampler. He glanced back to clear his tail and as he did, caught sight of six Japanese Kates, torpedo bombers, above and to his left.

He realized their intended target was the American shipping in the bay. He also realized with some panic that he was the only American pilot close enough to disrupt their torpedo run. As the Kates nosed over into a shallow dive, Hanson chased them in a low-side beam run gradually closing the distance to the nearest bomber, waiting patiently for the fuselage to swell and fill the orange ring of his gunsights, and when it did, he fired. The Corsair bucked fiercely as the shells rocketed out. The startled Japanese pilot immediately snapped out of his run and peeled off to the right. Hanson could see that the rear-turret gunner was firing at him, but he felt no hits.

Hanson pulled out of his dive, standing his craft on one wing, and swept up and around to the left in a wide circle for a high side run on the remaining Kates, which continued to drive inexorably down towards their targets. Below, klaxons sounded and sailors scurried for cover. A few puffballs of flak began to dot the sky, then gradually more. Hanson ignored the danger and fire walled—flicked the fuel mixture control to the full rich position and pushed the throttle home till it was flush with the asbestos shield, or fire wall—and with the resulting boost in power, quickly came around again and caught up to the bombers. He began fishtailing, using his guns in pairs to spray as many of the Kates as possible, in the hope of increasing his nuisance value. He knew very well that his only hope of stopping the attack lay in the possibility that he could unman the enemy pilots and make them break off.

Lower and lower they dropped. The sky was bright and cloudless, and no other planes were nearby. Hanson might almost have been putting on a demonstration except that the stakes were very high and everybody who might have been watching was scurrying for cover. Hanson's altimeter registered 5,000, then 4,000, 3,000, 2,000 feet. His long bursts were striking home, seemingly without effect. Not a single Kate wavered. The rear gunners were desperately trying to knock him off. Little puffs of smoke came out of their gun muzzles. Hanson was concentrating so intently on his attack he didn't see the tracers or feel the 7.7-mm. shell that struck home in the Corsair's engine. His thumb was jammed on the firing button, but the .50-calibre bullets, boresighted to converge at 300 yards, raised no smoke. Enraged and frustrated, he shouted, "Burn, why don't you burn?"

The shipping in the bay ballooned to target size and just as Hanson abandoned hope, the nearest Kate on the left side nosed over very slightly, then a bit more. Since a torpedo-bomber needs to come in very close at a low altitude to be effective, it was still too far short of the torpedo-release point to have been a deliberate maneuver on the pilot's part. Hanson grinned wolfishly and exulted as the Kate's dive became steeper and steeper. When it was clear to him the bomber was headed for the drink, he shifted his fire to the others, scourging them, riding closer and closer in the face of their answering fire. They were about halfway along their run when they finally

102

lost their nerve, and peeled off to the right, still in formation.

The few torpedoes they dropped fell harmlessly into the bay, to the cheers of sailors who had watched the tense struggle from their antiaircraft gun mounts. Hanson picked up the one Kate he had managed to flame and followed it all the way down, pecking at it with short bursts. He was close enough to see the rear gunner's face, which was ashen and incredulous. The Kate smashed into the water amid a burgeoning spume, and Hanson pulled out near the deck, skimming seaward. He had intended to chase the departing Kates, but his controls began to stiffen; he tapped the throttle. The engine roared, renewed, then began sputtering and a moment later, went dead. Hanson pumped the throttle, but there was no response. He turned the nose of the Corsair towards the outlying destroyer screening force. When it was still about five miles away, the plane lost altitude with a sudden lurch and Hanson made a dead-stick landing, bracing as the bay came rearing up to smack him. The Corsair slapped the water, skipped, came down again and pancaked along for about 20 yards, then nosed over into the drink. Almost immediately, it began settling. Unhurt, Hanson unsnapped his harness, scrambled out of the cockpit, jumped into the water, inflated his life raft and began paddling away, making for the destroyers. He was in high spirits. He had flamed three enemy planes which, together with the two he already had to his credit, made him an ace. He paddled industriously for almost five hours and finally was sighted by the destroyer *Sigourney* when he was still 250 yards off. As he drew closer, they could hear him singing at

103

the top of his lungs the popular song, "You'd Be So Nice To Come Home To."

Hanson had arrived just in time. Five minutes later, *Sigourney* and the other destroyers steamed south for Tulagi. Hanson had a marvellous time aboard the ship. He wrote his parents, ". . . rest yourselves. Healthy, happy, not hurt and three more Japs under my belt. That makes five and one probable. Say, the destroyer that picked me up was a brand new one. And boy, the swell chow!"

Two days later, Hanson caught the ferry to Guadalcanal, drew some gear to replace what he'd lost, and signed for a new F4U which he flew back to Barakoma Field, arriving on November 3.

"Welcome back," Major Owens said. "I expect now you'll be a little more careful."

"Yes sir," Hanson grinned mischievously. "I certainly will be more careful."

Hanson was not, however, temperamentally inclined to be cautious. His innate recklessness was a matter of comment among his fellow pilots. There was a rude, hard edge to his otherwise good-natured grin which, together with a fleshy pad beneath his eyes, making slits of them, mocked reason, restraint and common sense; or at any rate, earthbound common sense.

A survey undertaken by the Fifth Air Force to cull useful tips from top-ranking aces produced the consensus opinion that the most valuable trait in a combat flyer was aggressiveness. "Go in close and when you think you are too close, go in closer," advised Major Thomas B. McGuire, Jr. "Time and again," noted Colonel Charles H. MacDonald, "I have seen aggressive action, even from a disadvantageous position, completely rout a powerful Nip formation." Lieutenant Colonel Gerald R. Johnson agreed: "If your attack is sudden and aggressive, the enemy will be at a disadvantage regardless of his numbers and position. Do not wait; attack immediately and pick your targets with the intent to destroy." These words fairly well described Hanson in the heat of action.

His wingman on more than one mission, Lieutenant Sam Sampler, characterized him as "a demon." "No man on earth can stick with him," Sampler said. "He flies at top speed every moment, executing every known maneuver and then some. Sooner or later, Hanson is off by himself tackling huge formations of Zeroes."

Owens soon realized that, if anything, his newly-fledged sky hawk meant to be less rather than more careful. Owens fretted, and admonished Hanson, but to no effect. The young Marine pilot was, self-evidently, the sort of man who finds life a succession of challenges that have to be met head-on. Other pilots, during off-hours, swam lazily in the clear blue Pacific, but Hanson, for relaxation, picked up a diving mask and went 20 feet down in the waters off Vella Lavella, where sunlight gave way to murky shadows, to scrape for souvenirs in the battered hull of a sunken Japanese ship. Hanson knew the currents were treacherous and knew that an unfortunate roll of the wreck might pin him. It was, precisely, dangerous sport.

Combat aviation was a comparable sort of sport for Hanson. His flying mates often noted the extreme rigidity of his features during missions, and his obsessive chain-smoking in the cockpit, though he rarely smoked on the ground. They also marked the thrusting, implacable, relentless drive that set him apart in that scrambling arena of patriots and madmen—where a "kill" might have been cherished for a complex and not entirely healthy mix of reasons—as the most daring, most accomplished, most death-defying of the Marine flyers in the Solomons.

"For every Hanson," Major Owens said, "there are at least ten dead Marine pilots who tried to do only once what Hanson does every day."

Robert Murray Hanson was born on February 4, 1920, in Lucknow, India. His parents, the Reverend and Mrs. Harry A. Hanson of Newtonville, Massachusetts, were Methodist missionaries. Growing up in a land teeming with hungry and dispossessed millions and with the example of service provided by his parents' work, he had an opportunity to observe more, experience more, and grow more than the normal American boy. His rearing was so exotic that he didn't, in fact, even *see* a normal American boy until his junior high school years, when he came to the United States for the first time. His summers during this period were spent on his paternal grandfather's farm in Breckenridge, Minnesota, where, among other things, he took his first airplane ride. A barnstormer having landed his quilt-work jenny in a nearby pasture, the boy raced over, struck dumb with admiration and awe, and when the romantic figure with the helmet and goggles offered him a ride, he accepted eagerly.

Returning to India to complete his schooling, Hanson, always a good athlete, took up wrestling and went about it with the sort of determination that characterized everything he did. At the age of 18 he was a husky, well-muscled 180-pounder, and he took on and defeated men years older than himself to win the light-heavyweight wrestling championship of the United Provinces.

In the spring of 1938, it had been decided that Bob would return to the U.S. for his college education; he thereupon embarked on a bicycle trip through Europe as a means of gradually working his way back to the States, and seeing something of the world as well. He could hardly have picked a worse time. The continent was in a state of unrest, due to the threatening posture of the German Government which, under Adolph Hitler, fairly well represented the strain of rancor and bitterness and paranoia in an entire nation about to hurl itself over the precipice.

It was an ambiguous moment in history. Many people seemed to be living out a normal, carefree, peaceful season, but many others were preparing for war, and a host of innocents were already feeling its violence and terror. Hanson was in Vienna on March 11–12, 1938, when Austria ceased to exist. Along with thousands upon thousands milling in the streets—the Nazis jubilant, the anti-Nazis stunned and speechless—he heard the government of Kurt von Schuschnigg capitulate to Hitler's bullying demands. The Anschluss, the return of Austria to the German Reich, had been accomplished through muscle, backstage manipulation and brutal and unscrupulous pressures.

In the streets, hysterical Nazi mobs enjoyed themselves heaving bricks into Jewish stores. Swastikas, S.S. and S.A. uniforms appeared everywhere. Schuschnigg was replaced by the Austrian Nazi Seyss-Inquart. German troops poured across the border. "The fanatical eyes, the gaping mouths, the hysteria," wrote William L. Shirer. ". . . and the Austrian police! They were looking on, grinning."

Hanson was stupefied, a witness to the celebration and the brutality. He could hardly believe it was taking place in full view, without apology; Jews, liberal ministers, labor union leaders and government officials, ripped out of their homes and offices, taken under detention, later to be carted off to concentration camps. The memory of these scenes never completely left Hanson, nor did his rage. He'd had his first look at the enemy.

He returned to the United States and enrolled at Hamline University, in St. Paul, Minnesota, where he excelled in sports and was a fluent linguist, his languages being French, German, Spanish and Hindustani. To help support himself, he took an unusual job for a student, but one for which his skill as a wrestler and his sturdy physique well qualified him: he worked as a bouncer in a St. Paul night club.

The son of the owner of the club, James Gillis, was a licensed pilot. Gillis owned a Luscombe and often took Hanson flying on weekends and as a result, by the time the Japanese bombed Pearl Harbor Hanson already had acquired some proficiency as a flyer. He was then in his senior year, only a few months shy of graduation, but with typical impetuosity, he couldn't wait. In May, 1942, he enlisted for naval flight training. Four years earlier, he had seen the face of the enemy. It wasn't the language or the geography or the ethnic particulars of the face that mattered, but the arrogance and the lust, the viciousness, the idiotic joy of conquest, and Hanson had seen, up close, what that looked like, and it made his urgency immediate. He could appreciate, better than most Americans, what the fight was. Graduation seemed, by contrast, a puny goal.

Hanson won his wings and a Marine Corps commission on February 19, 1943. Four months later he arrived in the South Pacific with the Swashbucklers. In August he shot down his first two enemy planes. On November 1, he shot down three more and received a spot citation for the Air Medal from Admiral William F. Halsey.

In December, VMF-215 ended its tour and enjoyed a well-earned rest in Australia. Hanson had, by then, completed two tours. After the first tour he had been offered a rotation to the States and had turned it down. After the second tour he rejected the same offer, knowing full well that his experience made him much more valuable than any fledgling replacement could be.

"I came out here to kill Japs," Hanson explained with cold, unaffected bluntness. On the third tour, which for Hanson ran from January 13, 1944 to February 3, 1944, he did just that, at a rate unequaled and hardly approached by any other Marine flyer. Hanson flamed at least one enemy plane each time he flew a mission. He was credited with five kills on a single mission, twice credited with four. In the short space of 17 days, he destroyed well over a full squadron of Japanese planes.

Hanson's rise to eminence among Marine aces was so meteoric, and had such a sudden end, that the press services had no opportunity to publicize it, and as a result, Hanson had little of the notoriety accorded Boyington, Foss, Dick Bong and Tommy McGuire.

The rampage started on January 13. The full squadron, plus two flights of P-40's from Ondonga Field, New Georgia, flew an escort mission over Rabaul, their primary job being the protection of 18 TBF Avenger tor-

109

pedo bombers from Munda, which were scheduled to plant their ordnance on Lakunai drome.

The squadron rose very early for the short, one-hour hop to the newly-laid Torokina Fighter Strip #1 on Bougainville. (Seabees were then still working feverishly under sniper fire less than five miles inland to bulldoze two more strips out of the swamp and jungle around Piva Village.) Squadron 215 arrived at 7 A.M. for a pre-flight briefing, and had a light breakfast before departing at 9:30, minus two planes which had suffered accidents. The fighters rendezvoused with the Avengers ten miles west of Taiof Island and were on their way to Rabaul by 11 A.M., crossing the coast of New Ireland just north of East Cape, where a flight of enemy fighters picked them up and began making some harassing passes, looping, slow-rolling and buzzing in. There was a lot of feinting and jabbing but not too much earnest battle until the TBF's approached the target. By this time the enemy force had grown to 60 or 70 planes, most of them above and behind the screening Corsairs. On reaching Lakunai, the Avengers found the airfield covered by clouds and decided to hit the shipping in Simpson Harbor and Blanche Bay instead. They started their vulnerable bombing runs with the Corsairs tailing them and a swarm of Zeroes tailing *them.*

Hanson made his dive alongside a torpecker, then pulled out at 200 feet and checked his guns, expecting to be bounced by some Zeroes, feeling particularly vulnerable so close to the deck. The flak seemed unusually heavy to him. He winced at the buffeting the Corsair was taking as he scooted up to the rally point with the torpeckers, some of which were under attack. Hanson and his wingman, Lieutenant R.V. Bowman, ducked into a cloud, coming out on the New Ireland side, and drove up astern of a pair of Zeroes at 1,500 feet with their guns firing. Hanson's target burst into flame immediately but Bowman's banked and veered into a cloud. Hanson stood his plane on one wing, circling the cloud to pick up the damaged Zero but when it came out the other side it was already ablaze and on its way down. Hanson looked around for Bowman and, not seeing him, impatiently dropped down onto another pair of prime targets. One Zero split up and to the right, the other left and down, so as to cover each other's tails, a standard defensive maneuver which, in this case, didn't work. Hanson followed one into a cloud and chased it down to 300 feet, where he opened up and watched the tracers walk along the fuselage to the wingroot. Before Hanson could pull away, the Zero exploded. The pure white flash blinded him for an instant, just as the other Zero swooped down to attack. Quickly, Hanson whipped the Corsair back into the cloud and played footsie until he could see, gaining altitude all the while, and finally shook his assailant.

The sky was full of Zeroes, mostly from 3,000 to 6,000 feet, and as the TBF's retired over Rapopo drome, the flurry of dogfights intensified. Hanson bounced three Zeroes which were chasing a Corsair, forcing them to break off their attack. He feinted a chase then split-S down to join up on the F4U's, but they'd already scurried off. He hugged a spiraling cloud, twisting higher and higher, painfully aware that a low-flying Corsair going it alone was an easy mark for the fast, highly maneuverable Japanese planes. At about 3,000 feet he saw two Zeroes at 9 o'clock low. He glanced around quickly to see whether they were decoying for a larger force and, deciding they were not, dropped down on them before they could maneuver. His 45-degree deflection shot flamed one and he zoomed past them heading for the open water in the direction of New Ireland.

He was aware that he had already knocked down three Zeroes and, despite the extreme tension, felt jubilant. He was beginning to feel a knotting strain in his shoulders, however, and in the stiffness of his facial muscles. He decided it was time to head for home.

On the way, skirting clouds as he retired, he poked his nose out momentarily and saw a Zero dead ahead mushing along at well below 180 knots. He ran right up to him from astern and below, the tracers poured into the Zero's belly, and it burst immediately into flame. Hanson decided that must surely be the Zero's most vulnerable spot.

With four kills under his belt, he changed his mind about going home and made a few more passes at Zeroes as they scuffled through the sky, but without results. He was aware that the only planes he could see were enemy —all the Corsairs and P-40's seemed to have retired with the torpeckers. He decided to make just one final pass, on a Zero flying alone about 1,000 feet below him.

He no sooner started down than a pair of Zekes came up out of nowhere and latched onto his tail. He was diving steeply at great speed so he was able to keep the decoy's tail in his sights long enough to riddle it with shells and watch it flame at the wingroots and engine and turn lazily onto its back and go down before he had to break away to shake the Zekes. But they were good pilots and nothing Hanson tried worked. He clenched his teeth as the Corsair rocked for a moment—one of the Zekes had scored—then rammed the throttle forward and jumped into a cloud. As soon as his tail was in he slammed the rudder bar and jerked the stick hard in a violent right turn. He broke out of the cloud just as the Zekes flew into it, heading in the opposite direction. Grinning with satisfaction and with relief, he beat it for home, arriving about half an hour after the rest of the squadron, with seven 7.7-mm. holes in his fuselage.

He had flamed five planes on a single mission, which was a rare, if not entirely unique, performance. (The record of nine planes on a single mission was subsequently achieved on October 24, 1944, by Commander David McCampbell, who won a Medal of Honor for the feat.) Hanson was now a double ace. He acquired a new nickname, Butcher Bob, which wasn't all that flattering but was more accurate and more colorful than the official press corps nickname "One Man Air Force," routinely applied every few weeks or so to some pilot or other, to spruce up dull copy. The current front-running Marine ace was Pappy Boyington, who had, on January 3, knocked down three planes to bring his total to 28. This figure, which seemed beyond reach, was at least static, since Boyington had himself been flamed on that flight, and was missing in action.

Hanson's assault on this record was slowed considerably by bad weather which grounded him on two successive sorties. He next flew a mission on January 20. More than 50 fighters of all types—Lightnings, Warhawks, Corsairs and Hellcats—escorted 36 B-25 Mitchells on a bombing run to Vunakunau drome, and encountered a new wrinkle in air-to-air combat. The Zeroes were armed with phosphorus bombs which they tried to drop on the Mitchells. It was ingenious but totally ineffective.

Hanson flew close protection for the bombers in front

of their formation and did not attempt to break off to mix with an estimated 35 to 40 Zekes which were flapping about in search of stragglers. During the southwesterly retirement over the Warangoi River, he left the formation and went to the rear where a B-25 that had fallen behind was being pestered by a lone Zeke. Hanson came to the rescue and when the Zeke pulled away he followed, angling for a partial deflection shot. The Mitchell seemed already hurt as it continued out to sea, and was later to make a water landing off Cape St. George. Hanson pursued his target doggedly as it maneuvered from 3,500 to 5,000 feet, and finally drove a long burst into its right side. Hanson watched it fall off and hit the water just where the Warangoi met the coastline of New Britain. As he started up after the bombers, a Tony slipped in behind him. Hanson hurriedly put his nose down in a steep dive, and the enemy pilot hesitated before following, just long enough for Lieutenant G.M.H. Williams, one of the squadron's ten aces, to slice in and pick it off with a 45-degree deflection shot.

Two days later, on an escort mission to Rabaul, Hanson's thirst for adventure once again overcame him. During the retirement, he noticed a swarm of Zeroes, far beneath the flight altitude of 10,000 feet, driving in to assault the bombers from below. These Zeroes, which had apparently scrambled from Lakunai to defend against the Rabaul strike, had already knocked off one P-38 and two Corsairs from another squadron when Hanson dropped down to bounce them. He made two passes which were unsuccessful mainly because the pigeons decided not to play, then came down in a split-S to 1,200 feet and barreled into a formation of six Zeroes; the other American planes were then a good 8,000 feet higher up. The solo thrust flurried the enemy pilots so much they weren't able to answer his fire with any sort of discipline. One Zero tried to pull up but Hanson kept at him until he rolled over to the right and went into the water in a gaseous billow of flames. Hanson kicked rudder and pulled back on the stick, climbing. Repeating the same maneuver—a split-S and high speed dive—he perched atop two more Zeroes and when they broke, tailed the one which went up. As it pulled into a near-vertical climb, Hanson pulled up with it, his thumb joint white with the pressure of holding down the firing button. Finally the Zero caught fire and fell into a spin from which the pilot never recovered.

Expecting the other Zero to have been circling onto his tail, Hanson quickly slow-rolled, then climbed back up. Nobody was following. There had originally been six Zeroes, but the reckless lunge into their midst had completely shattered their formation and they had scattered. They were all over the sky. He saw a Tony diving to his right as he was climbing. He dropped his left wing and again split-S down, getting in a very long burst from stern. The Tony didn't pull up. He did a wingover and 'lled through—right into the water.

The three kills had raised Hanson's total to 14. He was nning to be talked about with more than modest re- in other squadrons, and his sometimes bizarre tactics analyzed; but as far as Major Owens was concerned, he was setting a bad example for the greener pilots.

"You can tell those young men for me to close their ears to any discussion of Hanson's tactics," Owens said. "He's a wonder. No one else can get away with it." Owens wasn't all that sure Hanson could continue to get away with it, and he told him so.

Hanson's standard reply was offhanded and disturbingly casual: "They've had plenty of chances. If they were going to get me, I'd be dead now."

The very next day, January 23, Hanson flamed four more Zekes, plus a fifth which he modestly claimed as a probable. Two he caught flying on their backs in an inverted attack on the bombers, which seemed particularly foolish to Hanson, as it exposed their tender bellies to attack from above; a third he flamed during the retirement, and the last, out to sea over the Duke of York Island. The probable was a Tony that dove away from Hanson trailing ribbons of smoke a couple of hundred feet behind, but the Marine hadn't actually seen him hit the water.

As usual, Hanson had flown away from his wingman early in the scuffle and did most of his fighting solo. This sort of hot rodding was looked upon with extreme disfavor by aerial tacticians, who put their chips on a two-plane element maneuvering in the extremely effective weaving pattern known as the Thach Weave, after Lieutenant Commander Jimmy Thach, a Navy carrier pilot who had first developed it back in 1942. No one, however, could argue with Hanson's effectiveness. Their concern was for his safety. Owens was especially concerned, since he had himself been flamed on that mission and had landed in the water with burns and cuts on his face and arms, later to be picked up and brought home by PBY Dumbos. He tried to convince Hanson that it could happen even to the best pilots, but Hanson was untroubled. "If they were going to get me, I'd be dead now."

He was, during this period, full of a nervous, jagged energy that seemed to leave him only when off duty.

After a flight, it took him longer and longer to simmer down, longer and longer before fatigue overtook him and he could sleep.

On January 25, flying TBF cover to Lakunai, he downed three Zeroes plus a probable fourth, for a total of 21. Hanson was in a rarified league, only the third Marine flyer to reach the double-ten plateau. For VMF-215 it was a particularly noteworthy sortie, as they lost no men and knocked off the grand sum of 22 Zekes and Tonys. Captains Donald Aldrich and Harold L. Spears, second and third to Hanson in the squadron, flamed three apiece, as did Captain Arthur Warner, who astutely noticed that the Japanese hadn't been quite so whimsical in introducing the phosphorus air bombs as the American pilots had thought. The bombs weren't primarily intended to blow up the Mitchells, but merely to mark their flight path, insuring that all Japanese fighters rising to intercept would be able to find them. Warner's suggestion to neutralize them was equally as clever: "Duplicate the bombs and send out small groups to lead enemy fighters in the wrong direction." But no record exists to indicate this gambit was ever taken up.

The next mission flown by VMF-215 was on January 27. Hanson, much to his dismay, was not scheduled. He was listed to take his regular turn as duty officer for the squadron, and none of his pleading had any effect on Major Owens. The C.O. adamantly insisted that Hanson take his turn on the ground.

"There will be other missions," Owens suggested.

"But our tour is almost up," Hanson begged. "I won't have too many other chances."

VMF-215 was, in fact, already scheduled to rotate back to the States. Hanson knew he wouldn't be allowed

117

to stay on for a fourth tour. After rotation and a thirty-day leave, he would most probably be assigned to instruct at a stateside training field. It seemed to him an anticlimactic end to a combat career. Not that he didn't also have other plans. He hoped to finish his final term at Hamline and "look around for a wife." Then he planned to return to India and hire on with a wealthy maharajah as a pilot. This, he felt, would eventually lead to his becoming a general in some Eastern satrap's air force. In any other man, this might have seemed a fanciful dream, but his squadron mates knew he was very much in earnest, and didn't doubt his eventual success. So they dubbed him The Maharajah of Rabaul, to go with his other, less regal title, Butcher Bob.

In any case, Hanson stayed home on January 27, and served his time as duty officer, and when the orders were cut for a mission on January 30, Hanson's name was on them. The squadron had, in the meantime, moved from Vella Lavella to the newly-laid forward strip at Piva, Bougainville, which was the operational nucleus for the increasing tempo of sorties aimed at reducing Rabaul to rubble. At Piva were squadrons of Corsairs, Avengers, Dauntless dive bombers, and a Royal New Zealand Air Force squadron of P-40 Warhawks. All of these, a total of 72 planes, left Piva early in the afternoon for Simpson Harbor.

Hanson had, as usual, eaten a light lunch consisting of a large bowl of salad and two or three heaping portions of canned fruit. Most combat flyers develop minor rituals or phobias to help prepare them for battle. Hanson's was the conviction that a meat meal made him sit too heavily to fly with agility.

The flight headed for the Duke of York Island, where the inevitable swarm of Zeroes intercepted, then crossed Rabaul Peninsula. The TBF's and SBD's attacked, scoring hits on four transports in the harbor. The flak was intense and fairly accurate, most of it at about 15,000 feet, where the high-cover Corsairs were mixing it with the Zeroes. Hanson saw an F4U plummet past with a Zero on its tail, and fell in behind. Both ships had been diving from a much greater altitude, however, and pulled far ahead. The Corsair maneuvered out from under, and when the Zero leveled out, Hanson crept up closer until finally he was in range. He pressed the red firing button, scoring hits from astern. The Zero began to kick rudder to get clear but Hanson followed the skidding maneuvers easily. Pieces of the Zero began to fly off into the slipstream. The Zero tried a turn. Hanson cut inside the circle and with a 15-degree deflection shot finished him off. Hanson climbed back up and swept wide of the Avengers, which were just then diving down for a second pass at the harbor shipping. As he was flying high cover, Hanson didn't dive with them. He swung into a cloud at 10,000 feet and climbed inside it, emerging 2,000 feet higher, behind a pair of Tojos, late-model Zeroes with improved flight characteristics. A scorching full-throttle thrust brought him within range before either of the Tojos spotted him. He opened fire from astern as soon as the rearward enemy plane ballooned to fill the orange gunsight ring. The Tojo took hits at the belly and went drifting slowly down in a graceful right spiral, a white flame burgeoning from the underside.

The other Tojo ducked into a cloud as Hanson reversed course with a half loop and roll out—an Immelman—to give chase. Losing the fast fighter in the clouds, Hanson zoomed out, climbed, reentered and came out on the other side. The Tojo, evidently unwilling to give battle, half-rolled and dashed for cover again. For several minutes, the two planes flirted through the pillar of cloud. The odds were with the Japanese pilot, since the hunter cannot see the intended victim's turns inside the cloud, but at 10,000 feet the thickness dissipated into puffballs of fleece in which the Tojo couldn't hide. Hanson caught him from astern. The Corsair shuddered as the .50-calibre shells left the six guns, at a rate of 80 per second, and the Tojo burst into flames at the left wing-root. Seconds later the wing sheered off, blowing back in the slipstream, and the dying fighter fell off to the right.

Hanson was very much aware that the three kills had brought his total to 24. He was chain-smoking and his teeth were clenched so tightly his jaw hurt. A liquid excitement began to flow through his body. Two more kills, he realized, would tie him with Joe Foss for second place in the Corps; and two more kills were a distinct possibility, since, as far as Hanson could see, the sky was full of Zeroes willing to engage.

Hanson drove up to the rally point, where a wild melee was in progress. Several passes at careening Zeroes scored no hits. He kept constantly flicking his head around to clear his tail, and at the same time, maneuvered for a setup. Executing a chandelle—reversing course with a climbing turn—he faced off against a diving Zero coming at him head-on. At a speed in excess of 800 miles per hour the two craft closed. Each pilot had only seconds in which to fire, before veering off to avoid a collision. As the distance narrowed, Hanson coolly held his fire. He could see the flickering small flames in the Zero's wings that meant he was firing. The Zero was, for an instant, in Hanson's sights. He jabbed the button. The two planes whooshed past each other and, as Hanson split-S down to pursue, the Zero burst into flames and tumbled uncontrollably down.

With his total at 25, Hanson was even more reluctant than usual to return home, even though there were few other American planes visible. He tried challenging a Zero, but the pilot thought better of it. He and another Zero spent several fruitless minutes trying to out-turn each other, then finally broke off. Hanson decided enough was enough. But on his way home, his frustration overcame him and he swooped down low over Cape St. George to strafe what he described as "a large house," actually a lighthouse.

Returning to Piva, the young pilot experienced a small foretaste of the sort of adulation America showered on her air aces. Service reporters interviewed him for promotional material and somebody very hastily put out a comic strip recounting his exploits. Sure to follow were frantic communications from stateside magazines advising their correspondents to get his story, particularly if he were to be put in for a high-ranking medal, which seemed likely. He had, after all, destroyed 20 enemy planes on six consecutive flights spanning a period of only slightly more than two weeks. And he was just the right sort of man for the popular news media to exploit. He was superficially an uncomplicated, affable, easygoing young American with sturdy if slightly puffy good looks. Best of all, the glory wouldn't go to his head. "Hanson is the least changed ace I've ever seen," said Lieutenant J. Edward Tyler, the squadron's intelligence officer. "No matter how many planes he gets, he's the same old Hanson."

The traditional hero's story never was written. On February 3, just one day before his twenty-fourth birthday, Robert Murray Hanson flew his last mission. For some reason the Zeroes and Tonys and Tojos didn't want to come out and play. Hanson scurried jaggedly across the skies, looking for action, but there was none to be had. During the retirement, several of the VMF-215 Corsairs descended on Cape St. George, on the southern tip of New Ireland, to strafe. The word strafe comes from the German verb *strafen*, meaning to punish, and in their frustration, the pilots no doubt meant to inflict some sort of punishment on any Japanese installation they could find.

The last person to see Hanson alive was Lieutenant Creighton Chandler of West Point, Mississippi, one of the squadron aces. According to Chandler, one of the squadron's F4U's, pilot unidentified, heeled over and dove down on the lighthouse.

"I saw the Corsair make a strafing run on Cape St. George, New Ireland," reported Chandler. All the pilots present noted the small volume of flak. It wasn't a particularly dangerous run. Chandler doubted the diving fighter was hit by antiaircraft fire. "But the Corsair pulled out too late. The plane's right wing struck the water, the gasoline tank burst into flames, and the plane somersaulted into the water. I dropped down low," Chandler added, "but could see nothing except pieces of debris."

Back at Piva Field, it was learned that Hanson was the only pilot who failed to return from the mission. To the others, his end seemed almost too ironic to be borne.

A master stylist, a pilot with such skill and finesse that his flying mates admitted they couldn't keep up with him, Hanson could not possibly have misgauged a simple strafing run so badly. Yet, apparently, he had.

Major Owens was especially disturbed. His eulogy was bitter with the knowledge that he had, in the final analysis, not been able to affect the dismal fate which Hanson had constructed for himself: "He wasn't afraid of anything. He took unnecessary risks, though. It was his only fault. He was probably trying too hard to top Foss and Boyington."

But he hadn't been dogfighting. He had been strafing a lighthouse, and lighthouses didn't count.

After he had been splashed on November 1, he had written his mother, "Don't give up hope if I am reported lost. There are many islands in this area and it is sometimes weeks before one can get out."

But the Reverend Hanson had had a premonition. Being the father of a war ace was a harrowing business. His premonition proved correct.

That afternoon a search mission went out to look for Hanson, consisting of pilots Spears, Burke, Cox and Sampler. They landed at 5:30 P.M. with a negative report. For a short time afterwards, VMF-215 flyers returning from sweeps over Rabaul retired via Cape St. George and swooped low to check the waters. There wasn't much point to it. It was mainly a sentimental gesture, from which even hard-bitten combat veterans are not exempt.

But unlike Pappy Boyington, who came out of a Japanese prison camp at the end of the war, Hanson never made it back from his last flight.

Lieutenant Commander A. Murray Preston receiving his Congressional Medal of Honor from President Harry S. Truman

5
A WONDERFUL
SHOW TO WATCH

~~~~~~

LIEUTENANT ARTHUR MURRAY PRESTON

Motor Torpedo Boat Squadron 33

SEPTEMBER 16, 1944

THE DECISION to assault and occupy Morotai Island was reached in the summer of 1944 by planners of General MacArthur's and Admiral Nimitz's strategy staffs, as part of MacArthur's "hit 'em where they ain't" tactic. Morotai was virtually undefended, whereas nearby Halmahera Island, the largest of the Spice Islands, held a complement of 37,000 men and boasted eight or nine airfields. The principle, simply stated, was to isolate such strong garrisons, leaving them to flex their muscles splendidly and irrelevantly while the storm center of the war leapfrogged past them toward Japan.

The landings on Morotai, on September 15, 1944, went unopposed. Not a shot was fired and only a handful of Japanese even showed themselves, the remainder having discreetly decamped to the hills, where they were to live out the war on berries and mountain water. The buildup of Morotai proceeded rapidly. Liberty ships arrived early on the sixteenth carrying heavy equipment to build an airfield, and a Navy base was established which included elements of Task Group 70.1, the motor torpedo boats of Admiral Thomas Kinkaid's Seventh Fleet, commanded by Captain S.S. Bowling. Skipper of one of the torpedo boat squadrons was Lieutenant Arthur Murray Preston, a thirty-year-old ex-lawyer from Washington, D.C.

A graduate of Phillips Andover Academy and Yale College, Preston had received a Bachelor of Law degree from the University of Virginia in 1938, and practiced law in the District of Columbia with the firm of McKenney, Flannery and Craighill until October, 1940, when he enlisted in the Navy's V-7 program and entered the Naval Reserve Midshipman's School at Northwestern.

The newly commissioned ensign, on March 14, 1941, reported for duty with Motor Boat Submarine Chaser Squadron 1. During the months prior to the attack on Pearl Harbor he went back into the classroom for special schooling on torpedoes and marine engines, and for the year and a half following, put that knowledge to use instructing in gunnery and torpedoes at Newport, Rhode Island. It wasn't until October, 1943, that Preston could look forward to some solid practical experience to supplement his theoretical expertise. Assigned to command of Motor Torpedo Boat Squadron 33, Preston sailed to New Guinea, reported to Captain (then Commander) Bowling and commenced combat operations in the Aitape-Wewak area.

On the day of the Morotai landings, the 7th Fleet Peter Tare squadrons moved up to establish a new base on that island. Among them was Preston's MTBron 33.

126

With almost a year of command under his belt, Preston was one of the senior squadron commanders, but by no means a seasoned veteran. By his own account, in fact, he was "still pretty green."

The first night, mosquito boat personnel slept aboard the tenders. Early the following morning, September 16, 1944, Captain Bowling went scouting for a suitable nest (base camp) for the PT boats. Preston, aboard the tender *Oyster Bay*, was relaxing in the wardroom when a radio message arrived from Rear Admiral Daniel Barbey, Commander Task Force 78.

"The Admiral wants the senior PT officer on board to report to him immediately," Preston was told.

Preston took a look around and, discovering that Captain Bowling was off the ship, realized the message was meant for him.

Grabbing a cap, he hailed the first boat at hand, which was PT 489, and went over to the flagship *Wasatch*, wondering what it could all be about. Admiral Barbey didn't keep him long in suspense. Immediately Preston arrived, the task force commander began to explain the situation.

"One of our pilots is down in Wasile Bay, Halmahera. He seems to be very near a Japanese garrison, and surrounded by heavy guns. A PBY has been driven off by artillery fire and the submarines say it is not a mission for them. That young fellow is in a very tough spot. I'd like to talk about the possibility of effecting a rescue with PT boats. What do you think?"

Preston sat down and cleared his throat. . . .

Earlier that morning, seven FM-2's (GM Wildcats) had taken off from the carrier *Santee* on the 5:15 A.M.

127

"Dawn Patrol" flight to strafe airbases on Halmahera. Strafing runs had, the day before, kept Japanese air from interfering with the landings on Morotai. This early morning mission had much the same purpose, guaranteeing that Japanese pilots refrain from giving way to any aggressive impulses they might have been harboring.

The mission went off smoothly, and on the return, one of the seven Navy pilots, twenty-four-year-old Ensign Harold Thompson of Lynwood, Washington, noticed some barges anchored in Wasile Bay. It was a target he could not resist. Gleefully, he flicked on his radio and announced his intention to strafe. Without waiting for an answer, he heeled his craft over and down in a steep dive from 10,000 feet. He had his thumb on the firing button and one of the barges in his sights when a heavy volume of antiaircraft fire opened up. Ugly blossoms bracketed the plane. At 6:55 A.M., a shell struck home.

"The next thing I remembered was being blown upwards and out," Thompson recalled. "The plane exploded. I looked down, saw the water, and pulled the ripcord."

According to a squadron mate, the plane disintegrated in midair and fourteen seconds after the chute opened, Thompson hit the water. Gasping, he struggled out of the harness. In the process, he discovered that his left hand was mangled and bleeding, three fingers ripped almost clean off. Clumsily, he tried to inflate his Mae West with his un-injured hand. He fumbled at the valve and sprang it; there was a hiss and a puff, and he felt himself pitching forward. The front part of the life jacket was ripped and useless. Bobbing up with rivulets of water coursing down his face, Thompson found himself tilted inexorably forward at almost a 45-degree angle.

He felt around in his pockets. The first aid gear was gone, evidently having been blown out by the concussive force of the shellburst, but by sheerest good luck, the sulfadiazine and morphine packets were floating in the water within reach. He applied the powder, then ripped the framing cord off a hand mirror and with his handkerchief managed to make a passable tourniquet.

At this point he looked around to take stock of his situation. He knew he had landed in Wasile Bay. He knew it was a Japanese garrison. Nevertheless, the shock of seeing Japanese shore guns and Japanese soldiers not 100 yards distant was great. He was severely disheartened. In his weakened condition, it occurred to him that the best course might to be to dog-paddle in to shore and surrender, but not ten minutes before, he'd been machine-gunning these very men. The quality of their mercy, he suspected, might be rather strained. He began to backwater nervously, wondering why Japanese troops weren't coming out to get him, and only then became aware that the other Wildcats of his Squadron were covering him by strafing the shore lines. Drifting past a jetty, Thompson saw some of their handiwork: four burning drums of oil and, oddly, two undamaged English bicycles.

It was gratifying, having his squadron mates standing by to provide air cover for him, but Thompson couldn't help feeling he'd had just about all the luck he was going to have. Soon the Wildcats would run low on fuel. They would have to leave. And where, in any case, was rescue to come from? He was smack in the middle of a Japanese strong point.

His feeling of hopelessness only increased when, at 9:20, a PBY Catalina flying boat came lumbering overhead. The pilot tried to set the cumbersome beast down but shore fire drove him away. It was clear that such an ungainly, slow-moving plane couldn't possibly survive inside the ring of Japanese guns. The pilot had to content himself with dropping a life raft which landed 50 yards off, and which the wind and tide carried Thompson's way. The wounded flyer inflated it and climbed aboard. To his dismay, he felt the rubber boat begin drifting towards shore. Paddling furiously, he managed to fight the tide and the boat coasted past the jetty, moving parallel to the shoreline at a distance of perhaps 50 yards, at which point Thompson noticed for the first time a 60-foot wooden lugger camouflaged with foliage, mostly palm fronds. He made for this boat and tied his raft to its anchor chain. Fortunately, the lugger was unoccupied. This protection from shore fire buoyed Thompson's spirits considerably. He flashed his mirror at the PBY, which acknowledged. Thompson lay back to wait developments.

At 10 o'clock, he glanced up at the sky and his heart sank. The six planes of his squadron were departing. Almost simultaneously, however, they were replaced by more planes winging in from the northwest, Hellcats from escort carriers *Sangamon* and *Suwanee*. The harsh drone of their engines was delicious music to Thompson's ears. He shouted in glee and scrambled to his knees.

The fighters pinwheeled down gracefully to spray the shorelines with a continual stream of fire. Thompson watched the Japanese gun crews scurry into foxholes as each Hellcat came screaming down, only to man their guns again when it pulled out of its dive. The scene

130

began to take on an unreal quality for the wounded man. The shock and loss of blood made him giddy and light-headed and at times he felt as if he were a detached observer of a larger-than-life-sized Punch and Judy show. He lay on his back and watched the clouds and the keening airplanes, heard the bullets whining and the shells exploding, and wondered dimly what it all had to do with him.

He had sensed, with the arrival of airplanes from the other fighter squadrons of Carrier Division 22 that the Navy hoped to rescue him. But for the life of him, he couldn't figure out how they meant to do it.

The conference aboard *Wasatch* expanded shortly to include Captain Bowling, who arrived from his reconnaissance with Lieutenant H.M.S. Swift, another of his squadron commanders. Admiral Thomas L. Sprague, Commander Cardiv 22, came in and took a seat. His airplanes were protecting Thompson. He wanted to see if the surface fleet could work out a plan to go in and pluck the downed pilot to safety. Throughout the conference, a number of men came in and out with messages or reports, adding to the sense of urgency. Various possible courses of action were proposed. Destroyers were suggested, and as quickly vetoed. The long, narrow entrance to Wasile Bay was known to be mined. Destroyers displaced 2,400 tons. They wouldn't do.

Shallow draft PT boats, however, wouldn't be subject to as great a danger from this source. In some respects they were ideal for a mission such as the rescue of Ensign Thompson. Small, agile craft powered by three 12-cylinder 1,200-horsepower Packard engines, they could make speeds in excess of 40 knots. A darting, high speed lunge into Wasile Bay and a rapid retirement were entirely feasible. On the other hand, the boats were lightly armed. They carried two pairs of .50-calibre machine guns and a 40-mm. Bofors, no match for the heavy shore guns known to be liberally sprinkled about the entrance to the bay. The four torpedoes, of course, would be of no use at all.

The boats were, in addition, not what one would call shell-resistant. The decks were of plywood, the sides and bottom planking two layers of 3/8 inch-mahogany. There was no armor. One direct hit from a 5-inch shell would easily demolish a mosquito boat. Even a miss close aboard could disable her.

Finally, and most important, the boats would be arriving in broad daylight on a clear, sunny day—and they were meant to operate under cover of darkness. The success of so obviously dangerous a mission was certainly in question, yet the consensus seemed to be that a successful rescue was, if not likely, then at least possible.

"They'll need air cover, of course," Captain Bowling said.

"Smokers as well as fighters," Preston added.

Admiral Sprague said, "I'm willing to go all out on this if there's any chance at all," and Admiral Barbey agreed it was worth a try. Preston then asked permission to make the attempt.

"Well, go ahead," Captain Bowling said, after a slight pause, "but don't for God's sake take any excessive chances."

They were all perfectly aware that the risk was great. Despite their high speed, the boats would very likely be under direct fire from heavy guns for periods upward of two hours. It was, in short, a mission Lieutenant Preston's subsequent citation would describe as "suicidal in its tremendous hazards." Not a man present but had gnawing doubts, and those upon whom responsibility weighed most heavily must surely have had disquieting thoughts about sending thirty men or more to bring back one. Yet the decision was made to go ahead. Communications were arranged which would tie the boats in to the air cover, and both boats and air cover to the base command. These details were swiftly agreed upon.

Preston already had PT 489 standing by. He briefed her C.O., Lieutenant Wilfred Tatro, on the way back to the tender, where he found PT 363 to be available. Preston then informed her skipper, Lieutenant (j.g.) Hershel Boyd, what was up, and the two boat crews were gathered together so Preston could ask them to volunteer, or decline, as they chose.

"I want to emphasize there won't be any criticism if anybody wants to stay on the tender," Preston explained, as the men, most of them seasoned veterans, listened impassively. "Now I'm going to shove off in a very few minutes, and I'm going to give the job a real good try."

Preston rounded up two more men he wanted along— the task force Intelligence Officer, Lieutenant Donald Seaman, and a medical officer, Lieutenant Eben Stoddard—and when they returned to the boats, the crews were standing by. So far as Preston could tell, nobody had begged off.

The flying circus put on by the fighter squadrons from escort carriers *Sangamon, Suwanee, Chenango, Fanshaw*

Bay and Thompson's own carrier, *Santee,* was so compelling a show none of the Japanese gunners took their eyes off it for a moment; they wanted to know *exactly* when a strafing plane would be heading for their positions. As a result, none were so distracted as to pay much attention to Thompson. At any rate, he was at no time the target of even random pot shots. The shore batteries fired only at the diving planes, which kept up a continuous strafing pattern, so there was never a letup in the destructive fire protecting the downed pilot.

Shortly before noon, Ensign William P. Bannister of *Suwanee*'s Fighter Squadron 60 gave his life in the effort to rescue Thompson. His Hellcat was hit by the ack-ack and plummeted into the bay not 100 yards from Thompson's raft. The plane was not burning but it did sink almost immediately. Thompson watched with horror and astonishment as the water enveloped the plane within seconds. Thompson prayed that Bannister would come bobbing to the surface, but he never did.

Moments later, Ensign Paul W. Lindskog, also of Fighter Squadron 60, took a hit and lost control of his plane. Thompson saw it careen out of view behind a mass of lush, tangled rain forest. Later he was to discover that Lindskog had managed to make a forced landing in the water clear of the area, subsequently to be picked up by the PBY Cat; but at the time, as far as he was concerned, he had seen two men killed for his sake and he despaired. Shocked out of his detachment, he began to tremble. The thing was getting out of hand. Not only was he weak from his wounds, he also was nauseated from having swallowed dye marker earlier. Guilt on top of that was a burden he couldn't bear easily. He closed his eyes and prayed it wouldn't happen again.

At 1:00 P.M., the two PT boats left Morotai, heading due south for 21 miles, then changed course to 220 degrees in order to make for the western shore of the narrow-necked entrance to Wasile Bay. The Japanese mines, it was assumed, had been laid primarily in mid-channel, and shore guns, according to Intelligence estimates, were most heavily emplaced on the eastern shore. Lieutenant Seaman, the Intelligence officer, told Preston there also *might* be guns on the western shore.

"We suspect there are guns there, but maybe not," Seaman said.

Preston said, "Well, we'll find out soon enough," and pored over the charts with the Intelligence officer to plan the best route into the inner bay. Wasile had much the shape of a left-facing long-necked swan caught in a vise and therefore short-rumped. Down in the gullet, like a stuck bone, was a long narrow island named Boebale.

"If there are guns on Boebale, that'll give us a lot of trouble," Preston mused. "But there's no avoiding it, I guess." Seaman nodded. Preston glanced back and watched the gun crew going about their business calmly, coiling ammo belts, checking and testing the guns. There seemed to be little anxiety and what little there was showed itself when, during lunch, one crewman muttered darkly, "The prisoner ate a hearty breakfast," and that remark was good for an overhearty round of laughter it wouldn't have gotten back at the base. However, the men ate well, showed none of the qualms they probably were feeling, and even managed a joke or two.

A few moments later, Preston sounded the buzzers for general quarters and had the boat skippers assign special lookouts to spot and report shell splashes. With the boats still four miles from the burgeoning land mass, a heavy gun estimated to be 90-mm. boomed out twice, straddling the boats, which was remarkably good shooting. Four more shots followed swiftly.

"There sure *are* guns on the western shore," Preston said.

"*Seem* to be," Lieutenant Seaman replied glumly.

The boats commenced zig-zagging and retired eastwards to open the range. Three pairs of guns from the eastern shore opened fire almost simultaneously. The boats flashed through the bay entrance on their dizzying course, the lookouts shouted above the deafening roar of the engines to call the splashes, and Lieutenant Seaman yelled, "Where are the guns? Anybody spotted the guns?"

"No, they're in the jungles," somebody yelled back.

At first the technique of "chasing splashes"—aiming the boat at the geysers of water raised by the splashing of shells, on the assumption that the gunners would change their range and deflection settings—worked quite well. It depended, of course, on knowing which gun had fired which shells, but after a while the bursts were so numerous they were hard to assign to a particular battery.

"Let's get out of here," Preston said. The boats took a 180-degree turn, spreading heavy, phosphorescent wakes behind them, and retired seaward. Preston was convinced the shore batteries were only minutes from scoring a hit. He didn't want to press his luck.

Seaman looked at Preston questioningly. Preston shrugged his shoulders. It didn't look promising. He was pretty well convinced by the reception committee that neither boat could survive in the narrows without strong air cover. One of the near misses had done some slight damage to PT 489, among other things blowing out a radioman's mike. Preston shuddered to think what a direct hit could do.

He visualized Thompson lying in the rubber raft, trapped in the inner bay, surrounded by a hostile enemy. He could imagine himself in Thompson's place: "If I were where Thompson is, I surely would want somebody to give it 'the old Sunday try' for me, so I'd have some assurance of a better prospect than decapitation or a diet of fish heads and rice for the rest of the war." But on the other hand, as Officer in Tactical Command, he had no intention of throwing away 35 lives for nothing.

Admiral Sprague had promised a dozen fighters and three VT smokers to support Preston directly and to strafe at his request. They hadn't shown up, nor could they be raised on the radio. Without them, Preston thought regretfully, he'd have to follow Captain Bowling's order to not take excessive chances.

As the day wore on, Thompson became accustomed to seeing his air cover go through an aerial changing of the guard. At noon, Hellcats from Fighter Squadrons 26 (*Santee*) 35 (*Chenango*) and 60 (*Suwanee*) took their place in the rotation. Thompson tried to count them but there were too many and he found himself counting the same ones twice. He was, anyway, having difficulty concentrating. He was hungry, thirsty, and dizzy, and the sun and salt water hurt his eyes.

He ached for deliverance. At the same time, he wished everybody would go away and leave him alone. He fought his self-pity, but at random moments found it overpowering. Every fighter pilot flew with death on every combat mission. Each man in his own way came to terms with that ugly fact. But in this case, Thompson had been lying helplessly in his raft for more than five hours, growing weaker and more sickened, and time itself was an enemy.

The PT boats, out in the open water, streaked about to evade the ranging shots of the heaviest guns, while Lieutenant Seaman continued his efforts to contact the promised Hellcats. After perhaps ten minutes of this, two of the lookouts reported fighter planes over Halmahera, and Lieutenant Seaman, popping up for a looksee, said excitedly, "That's Hatetaboko drome over there. They may be Jap planes." The ominous specks grew larger. The gunners tensed at their Bofors. A moment later, everybody was vastly relieved when the planes turned out to be the overdue air cover, 12 fighters from *Suwanee* and 3 smokers from *Sangamon*. Seaman tried the radio once again and this time raised Lieutenant (j.g.) George Stouffer, who was flying one of the smokers.

Stouffer told him they knew exactly where Thompson was and offered to lead the boats directly to the downed pilot. Preston accepted with alacrity.

The Hellcats peeled off and began strafing the gun positions on both shores. The boats followed close behind, running at full throttle. After due deliberation, Preston had decided to make the run in down the middle of the channel, despite the mines. The danger was great, but there was a chance the shallow-draft boats could ride over the mines, whereas the battery fire was so accurate that Preston felt it absolutely necessary to open the range from both shores as much as possible.

The strafing reduced the volume of hostile fire somewhat, but not completely, and as the two torpedo boats roared into the narrows, shell bursts consistently straddled them at distances of 50 to 75 yards, close enough to rock the frail plywood boats, sending spray washing over the decks and wetting down the crews. They also could hear the ugly swish as shrapnel passed overhead, and this made them feel particularly vulnerable.

PT 363 was then on station 50 yards directly behind PT 489. The boats zig-zagged slightly and approached the lower end of the narrows. To the right, Preston could see Cape Patjikara, which was not a cape at all but a pouting lip of land extending from the rain forest, and to the left Lolobata airdrome. There were 5-inch guns at both places. These cannon took them in their sights and began a punishing cross fire. On the radio, Lieutenant Seaman asked if the air cover could pinpoint specific shore guns. "We can try," was the reply. Seaman thereupon called the fighters down on the 5-inchers and they obliged by silencing them.

Passing the airfield, the boats closed rapidly on Boebale Island, which sat astride the channel, cutting it into two narrow lanes. There were at least two heavy guns on Boebale. The Hellcats took them under especially intensive fire and the boats roared through the easterly channel, approaching Lolobata Point. Another heavy calibre gun challenged them there and the strafing concentrated on it, but the gun persisted. The boats zig-zagged erratically as each shot boomed out, the shells consistently landing in their wakes. This was very threatening. The boats couldn't evade indefinitely. Preston shouted for Seaman to ask for smoke and a moment later, Stouffer came down to 100 feet, about 200 feet offshore, trailing a fluffy, billowing smoke bank which completely shielded the boats from shore view. Seconds later, the boats themselves passed into the screen and had to run blind for long moments. Bursting through to the other side, they found themselves finally in the inner bay. For a blessed moment, there were no shore guns to take them in range.

The lookouts craned their necks but nobody was able to see Thompson or the life raft, or even the lugger he was reportedly tied to. The boats came around Lolobata Point, turned east, now running along the length of the smoke screen, which was in the shape of a loaf of French bread, and throttled down so Preston could get his bearings. Reaching the end of the smoke screen, they found themselves at point-blank range of several Japanese guns which fortunately were, just then, busy defending themselves from the assaults of the air cover.

It was obvious that, even with twice the firepower supporting them, the boats couldn't stay where they were. Preston eyed the closest enemy gun, about 100 yards inshore from a jetty. He shook his head. *Impossible.* If that was where Thompson was, it was hopeless. While PT 363 took station about 100 yards offshore and commenced strafing the beach, Preston called for a second smoke screen to buy some time. Lieutenant (j.g.) Dwight Long came down and deposited a dense screen beginning directly on the Japanese gun, past three barges and the jetty, behind Thompson's lugger to a second pier farther down the "swan's back."

The boats spent some minutes roaring around looking for Thompson, but unsuccessfully. Preston was about to burst with frustration when Lieutenant Stouffer zoomed low over the boats and made a pass on the lugger, dropping a smoke pot alongside Thompson's raft. PT 363 continued strafing the beach while, under cover of this fire, PT 489 turned and approached the lugger, and Preston was overjoyed, finally, to spot the downed pilot.

As the boat nosed in, the men manning the guns closely watched the palm fronds used to camouflage the lugger. For all they knew, the foliage might also be concealing Japanese guns. Lieutenant Seaman pushed past a group of sailors and peered over the side at the life raft. Some of the men were yelling encouragement to Thompson but he wasn't reacting as they'd expected. He didn't even look particularly happy. Liuetenant Eben Stoddard, the medical officer, said, "I'm not sure he can make it by himself, he looks to be in bad shape."

Thompson had responded to the din of the PT boat engines by struggling to a sitting position. He was only dimly aware that rescue was at hand. He could see that the faces smiling down at him were American and he could hear them yelling at him but the boat was about ten yards off and in the engine's bedlam he couldn't make out the words. He had an idea they wanted him to do something but he couldn't figure out what.

On the bridge, Preston and Lieutenant Tatro were discussing whether the boat could get in close enough to throw Thompson a line without either swamping the raft or banging up against the lugger when Lieutenant Seaman and Motor Machinist Mate Charles D. Day took matters into their own hands.

Seaman realized somebody would have to go over the side and bring Thompson in, so he shrugged off his shoulder holster and pulled off his shoes. As he was about to dive overboard, Motormac Day came up out of the engine room and indicated he was coming along. Seaman waved him away but Day wasn't to be put off. He got out of his shoes and followed Seaman over the rail. They swam over to the raft, Seaman holding it steady while Day scrambled aboard to untie it. Thompson was smiling tentatively but otherwise made no comment. Seaman asked him if he could move. Thompson shook his head. Day slipped back into the water and, together, he and Seaman towed the raft back to the PT boat, where waiting hands lifted Thompson aboard. In a state of semi-shock, the dazed and damaged pilot began mumbling something, but they were too busy hustling him into a comfortable berth in the cabin to listen. Lieutenant Stoddard followed and immediately began tending his wounds. The time was then 5:15 P.M. Thompson had been trapped in Wasile Bay just over ten hours.

Throughout all this, both boats maintained heavy strafing fire on the beaches. With Thompson safely aboard, they turned their 40-mm. Bofors on the Japanese lugger which had given him protection, an unsentimental gesture that nobody thought at all inappropriate. The wooden lugger burned briskly before six shots had been fired, settling into the water even before the PT boats had gotten out of sight.

Retiring westward, the boats headed back towards Lolobata Point. Lieutenant Long's smoke screen, behind them, still frustrated the shore guns emplaced near the jetties, but the screen laid earlier by Lieutenant Stouffer was coming apart in the breeze. The solid front had rents in it through which shore batteries began firing. As if enraged that the prize for which the immense struggle had taken place might be denied them, the gunners redoubled their fire, chasing the erratically veering mosquito boats with unnervingly near misses. The concussion shook the boats and threatened to hurl the men to the decks. Ranging shots preparatory to full battery fire had the boats nicely bracketed and rapid range and deflection changes inched the splashes closer. In the cabin, Lieutenant Stoddard had to hold onto Thompson to keep him from falling out with each violent zig-zag of the boat. Seaman got on the radio and pleaded with the air cover to lay another screen. Lieutenant Aaron Katz, one of the three smokers, made a pass and with great finesse put a second layer on the original screen. It reminded one of the eyewitnesses of a pastry chef's elegant froths of cake frosting.

The mosquito boats roared past Lolobata Point and turned north into the narrow channel. Lieutenant Preston told Seaman to ask that all the available fighters cover the run home, a request that proved unnecessary since they were already beginning a ferris wheel pattern of passes that had one plane pulling out of its dive, two more hurtling down with their wing guns flashing, a fourth just peeling off and the remainder queueing up and patiently waiting their turn. Preston found himself gaping. In addition to firing the .50-calibre machine guns, the Hellcats were dropping bombs and a few even had rockets, which whooshed out ahead to score the shorelines. The rate of fire, Preston recalled, was of "almost unbelievable intensity."

The boats raced the length of Boebale Island, came

abreast of Cape Patjikara and careened past Lolobata drome. Those who peered back could see a fuel dump burning. They heard an ammo locker exploding fitfully, a random grace note in the symphony of violent sounds. Preston sensed that the volume of answering shore fire had diminished somewhat. This was because four of the heavy guns had been silenced by the air cover, without whom, Preston acknowledged gratefully, the mission would have been nothing short of madness.

The shore batteries fired their last few rounds, more in frustration than with any hope of success, when the boats were five miles out to sea. Preston looked at his watch and noted the time at 6 P.M. They had been under fire for almost three hours, had sustained no casualties on either boat, and had picked up their man. He went down to the cabin to visit Thompson. The wounded man was conscious, wrapped in blankets so only his head showed, and it was a haggard, spent face that Preston saw. The eyes were open but not focusing too well. Thompson's lips trembled and he smiled gratefully, but he said nothing. Preston thought about the enormous effort that had gone into the rescue. There had been more than 50 planes involved at one point or another, two PT boats and countless base personnel in support. At that moment it certainly seemed worthwhile.

He patted Thompson on the shoulder and left so the flier could get some sleep. Topside, there wasn't any overt hilarity, but he had the sense that the men were feeling very good. They were relaxed and cocksure and proud. He felt some of that himself.

The boats arrived at Morotai and came alongside the tender *Oyster Bay* at 7:30, after an uneventful run

144

home. Thompson was immediately transferred to the tender's sickbay. The crews stood around watching the transfer, responding with some slight embarrassment when Thompson waved at them weakly, a sort of half salute, then cleared their throats and set about cleaning up. The boats would have to be in shape for the next mission, whatever it might be.

Four days later, Thompson was aboard the escort carrier *Santee*, recuperating. *Santee*'s skipper, Captain R.E. Blick, asked him what he thought of the stirring rescue.

"Well," said Thompson, evidently unable to recapture the tension, stress and pain, and happily recalling only his gratitude, "it sure was a wonderful show to watch."

Lieutenant Commander Eugene B. Fluckey aboard the U.S.S. *Barb*

6

LIFE BEGINS
AT FORTY...FATHOMS

≈≈≈≈≈≈≈≈≈≈≈≈≈≈≈≈≈≈≈≈≈≈≈≈≈≈≈≈≈≈≈≈≈≈≈

LIEUTENANT COMMANDER EUGENE FLUCKEY

U.S.S. Barb

JANUARY 23, 1945

Submarines had an effect on World War II altogether disproportionate to the size of the force. The Silent Service comprised less than two percent of the U.S. Navy, yet accounted for 1,314 Japanese merchant and naval vessels sunk, some fifty-five percent of the total of Japanese losses. This score included large warships (such as the aircraft carrier *Soryu*, sunk by *Nautilus*; the 31,000-ton battleship *Kongo*, sunk by *Sealion II*, oil tankers, freighters, transports, smaller men-of-war and miscellaneous ships of 500 gross tons or more. It did not include a large number of sampans and junks which had the misfortune to get in the way of the serious business of war.

In addition to the heavy loss in cargo carriers—which the Japanese shipbuilding industry couldn't replace at anywhere near the rate necessary to maintain a viable merchant fleet—the loss of convoy routes further guaranteed the collapse of the war effort. Without petroleum, crude iron, raw rubber and rice from Southeast Asia, Japan soon found it impossible to sustain the military machine or adequately to feed the hungry civilian population. By the end of 1944, the Japanese Total Mobilization Bureau conceded that "if the resources of the south, especially petroleum, are abandoned, with the passage of time we will lose our ability to resist attack." Thus the purely military operations of the submarine service proved to have far-reaching geopolitical repercussions.

American submarines by no means restricted themselves to direct assaults on the enemy, however. The versatile "pig boats" also performed photo reconnaissance, supply, transportation and evacuation missions. They served as floating weather stations, marker beacons, picket ships, and they rescued many a downed aviator from a hostile sea, frequently in enemy-held territory. They landed coast watchers and intelligence agents. Often they were the only means of supplying guerrilla units fighting behind enemy lines. Among the numerous undersea passengers, at one time or another, were: 13 Army and Navy nurses evacuated from Corregidor by *Spearfish*; Carlson's Raiders, on their way to and back from the raid on Makin Island aboard *Nautilus* and *Argonaut*; and a boatload of refugees which *Nautilus* carried from Bougainville to Australia, including 14 nuns, 3 married women and 3 squalling babes-in-arms. Probably the most valuable cargo of the war was used by *Trout* as ballast: twenty tons of gold bullion and silver pesos, originally from Manila bank vaults. (This fortune was not distributed to the crew at the end of the patrol, as one rumor had it. It was shipped to the U.S. for safekeeping.)

Seven submariners won Medals of Honor, all in the Pacific theatre: Captain John Cromwell and Commanders Howard Gilmore, Sam Dealey, Richard O'Kane, George Street, Lawson Ramage and Eugene Fluckey. Three of these awards, to Cromwell, Gilmore and Dealey, were posthumous. A fourth, to O'Kane, was awarded at war's end, O'Kane's submarine *Tang* having been sunk by one of her own torpedoes which had porpoised and made an erratic, circular run, and nine survivors, O'Kane among them, having been taken prisoner by a Japanese destroyer.

Fluckey's award was by no means his first citation for "extraordinary heroism." He had, in fact, already won three Navy Crosses, one for each of his first three war patrols as skipper of the submarine *Barb*. An audacious and aggressive pursuer of enemy vessels, the red-headed, freckle-faced young naval officer was considered by his peers to be one of the titan submariners of the war. According to Chief Gunner's Mate Paul Saunders, who was a "plank owner" of the *Barb*, having served on every one of the sub's patrols, the crew commonly referred to their skipper as "Gene," which was, in its offhand way, a clear mark of affection and an intimation of the trust they accorded the man whose skills determined whether they would live or die.

Eugene Bennett Fluckey was born in Washington, D.C., on October 5, 1913. He entered the Naval Academy in 1931, graduated four years later, and was assigned to the battleship *Nevada*. Submarines, however, were his first love, and he lost no time transferring to that service arm. At the outbreak of war, he was serving aboard *Bonita*, already qualified for command of submarines. Following further schooling, he reported to Commander Submarine Force, Pacific Fleet, Admiral Charles Lockwood, was assigned to *Barb* as Prospective Commanding Officer for one war patrol and on April 27, 1944, assumed command.

His crew soon discovered that, though moderately shy and given to a great deal of affable grinning, Fluckey had no intention of hanging back when action was in the offing. He drove himself and his crew to the limit of their capabilities, was demanding as a skipper, yet never inaccessible, and the result was a proud submarine with an exemplary war record.

During her first three war patrols, *Barb* sank a large number of enemy ships, including the 22,000-ton aircraft carrier *Unyo*, and participated in a noteworthy rescue operation in the midst of a raging typhoon. This occurred during her second patrol, which had begun rather inauspiciously, with a bird perched on the periscope and refusing to fly off. The perplexed young skipper banged and shook the scope, cursed and hooted at the bird, but it wouldn't depart. Fluckey glared at it through the auxiliary periscope. The bird airly ignored him. As the impasse threatened to persist indefinitely, Fluckey graciously conceded defeat and submerged, concluding that the bird was "the latest fiendish antisubmarine weapon of the Japs."

That was on August 31, 1944. One day later, *Barb*, and her wolf pack mates, *Queenfish* and *Tunny*, were bombarded by enemy planes, *Tunny* being damaged so badly she had to bow out and return home. Two more weeks passed, during which time Fluckey became more and more convinced that the patrol was destined to be a total fizzle. On September 14, *Barb* attacked a *Chidori* class destroyer escort, the torpedoes missed, and the grim chase that ensued was not calculated to reassure any skipper's misgivings.

Two days later, *Barb* received a report from ComSub-Pac describing one of those tragic ironies which abound in wartime. A wolf pack consisting of *Growler*, *Pampanito* and *Sealion* had, shortly after midnight, September 12, made radar contact with a large, well escorted Japanese convoy in the South China Sea. The wolf pack tracked the convoy throughout the night and into the day, periodically making torpedo attacks, and in the process sank the frigate *Hirado*, the destroyer *Shikinami*, and several transports and freighters.

One of the merchantmen, the *Kachidoki Maru*, had in her holds 750 British and Australian prisoners of war, most of whom had been captured when Singapore fell in 1942. Another, the *Rakuyo Maru*, carried an additional 1350 PWs. These 2,100 men were the hand-picked survivors of an original work force of more than 20,000 PWs who had completed a railway line from Mandalay to Saigon for the Japanese; some thirty months of hard labor. They suffered from pellagra, beriberi, dysentery, edema, malaria and ringworm, to name only the more common of their maladies. They were going to Japan to work in the Emperor's mines and factories, a grim thought for men already worked half to death.

None of them were destined to arrive, however. On the night of September 12, torpedoes from Commander E.T. Reich's *Sealion* sank *Rakuyo Maru* and torpedoes from Commander P.E. Summers' *Pampanito* sank *Kachidoki Maru*. Many of the Allied prisoners, having survived more than thirty months of bitterest gall and brutality, were scalded, drowned, or crushed to death. Some, more fortunate, broke out of their holds and followed the Japanese across the yawing decks of the sinking ships to hurl themselves into the dark sea.

Shortly afterwards, a Japanese destroyer doubled back to pick up survivors. Some of the Britons and Aussies swam to the escort ship and tried to board her, only to be driven off with pistols. The destroyer picked up the Japanese survivors, then steamed off, leaving behind perhaps 200 or 250 prisoners, bobbing helplessly in an oily, debris-strewn sea. Nearly all were covered with the crude oil that coated the surface of the water. Only a few had life belts, and many had been injured by underwater explosions. Dazed, alone, with no hope of survival, they watched the fiercely burning *Rakuyo Maru* circle aimlessly throughout the afternoon until finally she sank amid a billowing of smoke and with great hissings of steam and crackling noises.

The survivors floated on the surface of the sea for endless hours, burned by the sun during the day and chilled at night. All had running sores from the salt water. They managed to catch some rain water and a few fish, but they were terribly hungry and thirsty, and were sustained only by whatever it is that keeps men striving against all reason. Then, finally, on the afternoon of the fifteenth, through ravaged eyes, they saw what appeared to be a mirage. Not very far distant, a submarine was rising out of the sea.

Pampanito and *Sealion*, having followed the Japanese convoy almost to Hong Kong, finally gave up the chase and turned around, passing by the greatest good fortune through the very waters where the diminishing numbers of survivors bobbed. Commander Summers spotted the first group of fifteen men aboard a raft and made for them, assuming them to be Japanese. "The men were covered with oil and filth and we couldn't make them out," Summers reported, "but black, curly hair didn't look like Japs." The castaways began shouting, in English.

"Pick us up *please*," they cried. "Pick us up *please*."

Realizing immediately what must have happened, Summers and Commander Reich began rescue operations in a hectic race against the onfall of darkness, by which time *Pampanito* had rescued 73 men and *Sealion*, 54. There were still many survivors in the water, but neither submarine could safely accommodate an additional man. However, there was a sliver of hope for those left behind. A message had been flashed that morning to Admiral Lockwood, who had transmitted the call for help to *Barb* and *Queenfish*, which were then some 450 miles distant. Both of these submarines responded immediately.

It was while en route towards the PWs that *Barb* stumbled across a Japanese convoy of tankers escorted by destroyers and the aircraft carrier *Unyo*. Aware that every moment he delayed might very well cost Allied lives, Fluckey paused only momentarily for a single torpedo attack which netted the prime target plus a tanker, then sped at top speed for the survivor area.

"There is little room for sentiment in submarine warfare," Fluckey retrospectively noted in his log, "but the measure of saving one Allied life against sinking a Jap ship is one which leaves no question, once experienced.

I would forego the pleasure of an attack on a Jap Task Force to rescue any one of them."

Unlike *Pampanito* and *Sealion*, *Barb* and *Queenfish* had time in transit to prepare for receiving passengers. "By the time we arrived in the area on September 17, we were ready to accommodate a hundred men," recalled Fluckey. But the survivors had been in the water almost five days, and the sea had claimed still more of them. *Queenfish* was able to pick up only 18, *Barb*, only 14. Many of these were too weak to help themselves aboard. Some were too dazed even to realize that rescue was at hand. *Barb*'s Torpedo Officer, Jim Lanier, dove over the side and secured lines around the survivors' waists. Motor Machinist Mate C. S. Houston joined him. On *Barb*'s deck, the sub having been flooded down and the bow planes rigged out, other crewmen hauled the survivors aboard.

They came out of the ocean like primitive sea beasts, dripping water, oil, muck, and slime, and stood patiently, sucking on water moistened pieces of cloth while their clothes were scissored off. A gang of "Cleaners" then washed the coating of drab green crude oil from their bodies with light hydraulic oil, following which they were passed below by the "Transportation Gang" for medical attention. Pharmacist's Mate William Donnelly and his six volunteer nurses washed their eyes with boric acid solution and a few drops of mineral oil. Those most in pain received morphine shots. Most of the rescued men had conjunctivitis from the crude oil. Donnelly instilled yellow oxide of mercury. He fed them sweetened water in tablespoons, and bits of chipped ice, and after a while, hot coffee laced with a bit of brandy. This, he

154

found, seemed to make them rest more easily. "Sleepers" led them to the forward torpedo room, to be berthed in the torpedo racks.

Donnelly worked tirelessly from 7:45 in the morning until midnight, his work made more difficult by the typhoon that was building up. Soon *Barb* was at a 20-to-30-degree roll and most of the survivors, even the seasoned seamen among them, became seasick.

Topside, Fluckey ordered his men into lifebelts. The sea had begun to lash the submarine, frothing up through the wooden deck gratings, making footing treacherous. Small black scud clouds floated overhead. Soon it began to rain, and *Barb*, rolling violently, fought up and down the deepening troughs. Two more survivors were spotted. Lieutenant Commander Bob McNitt and Motormac Houston dove over the side and brought them aboard. Huge waves broke over *Barb*'s hull. At times, her nose dipped and the propellors at the stern turned in thin air. The winds increased from 20 to 50 knots. Fluckey cleared the decks, the members of the rescue party crowding onto the bridge to continue operations. As the afternoon wore on, it became increasingly evident that no more men would be rescued, but Fluckey doggedly persisted.

"*Barb* pitched and rolled so violently that we on the bridge could do little other than hang on," Fluckey later wrote. "The wind shrieked and tore at the rain hoods which protected our heads. Every other wave broke over us, pounding tons of green sea water on our backs. In between waves, the rain, whipped by the 100-knot winds, blistered our faces."

Soon darkness fell, and it was no longer possible even

155

to see the bow of the ship from the bridge. Fluckey ordered the searchlight turned on, and the rescue operations continued, though in vain. The radar officer, Lieutenant Dave Teeters, tried to pick survivors up on his radar screen, but this effort also proved fruitless.

By dawn the following morning, the typhoon had abated somewhat. The winds were down to 35 knots. *Barb* spent that entire day searching without success for additional survivors; there were many bodies, Allied and Japanese, but no living men. At 7 P.M., *Barb* set course for Tanapag Harbor, Saipan. On that five day trip, most of the survivors recovered rapidly, with Donnelly feeding them multi-vitamin capsules, concentrated milk, water and hot tea to begin with, then on the second day, broth, soft-boiled eggs and fruit juices.

"I take back all I ever said about you Yanks," one Aussie sighed.

And another, "Three bloody years without a drink of brandy, please give me more."

One man, with tears in his eyes, wrung a friend's hand and cried, "Matey, we're in safe hands at last."

The survivors were dressed in donated clothing, and aboard *Barb*, the open hearted crewmen went even further. They contributed more than $300 as a stake for the PWs, a sum that included nearly every penny aboard ship. *Barb* arrived at Tanapag Harbor on September 25. The rescued men were transferred to a hospital ship, the U.S.S. *Fulton*, and from there to the Army's 148th General Hospital. In all, 159 men had been picked up by the four submarines, and of that number seven died en route.

Most of the survivors were strong enough to make the

transfer unaided, but a few required stretchers. The sub crews lined the decks to wave goodbye, and there was a great deal of handshaking.

One man, with haunted eyes, reached out to pluck at Fluckey's sleeve.

"God bless you, Captain," he said.

Fluckey turned away. He had a lump in his throat and wasn't able to reply.

That patrol, Fluckey's second as skipper of the *Barb*, ended on October 3. The next patrol, from October 27 to November 25, added 28,000 tons of merchant shipping to *Barb*'s total, which was then one of the highest in the service. The patrol that followed was even more successful, primarily due to Fluckey's growing conviction that there was almost nothing his submarine couldn't do.

On the night of January 23, 1945, in a pretty fair imitation of a PT boat, she entered enemy-held Namkwan Harbor on the China coast in pursuit of a Japanese merchant ship which had, during the previous two weeks, successfully eluded American wolf packs. It was the exploit for which Fluckey was to win his Medal of Honor. *Barb* recklessly nosed into enemy waters and what followed was, in the words of Admiral E.W. Grenfell, "one of the great stories to come out of this war—when it can be told."

The great adventure actually began two weeks earlier. On January 8, *Barb*, *Queenfish* and *Picuda*, constituting a wolf pack, sighted a Japanese convoy off Tungyung Tao, at the north end of the Formosa Strait. The wolf pack patiently tracked the eight freighters and their escorts for more than four hours, then made a daylight periscope attack. *Barb* fired six torpedoes, four of which struck home, sinking a transport and a freighter and damaging a cargoman. The third explosion was unusually loud.

"Now that's what I call a good solid hit," Fluckey said distractedly, intent on preparing the setup for a coming stern salvo.

Behind him, a seaman muttered, "I'd hate to be around when he hears a *loud* explosion."

He was wryly referring to the fact that the force of the explosion was threatening to sink the attacker. The concussion slammed into *Barb*'s hull, shattered light bulbs in the conning tower, burst open cases of canned goods in the forward torpedo room, and ripped a section of deck grating off the superstructure. Crewmen had to grab for support to keep from being hurled to the deck, as the sub was forced sideways and down by the great pressure, yet Fluckey was so intent, he hadn't, at first, noticed anything amiss.

The victim had evidently been an ammunition ship. When Fluckey peered through the scope a moment later, only a pillar of smoke remained. The stern of the transport was sticking up at a 30-degree angle, preparatory to sliding below, and the cargoman was on fire amidships at the water line. Several escorts dropped back to challenge the attacking submarines whereupon there ensued a lengthy game of cat-and-mouse while the freighter steamed ahead, zig-zagging erratically.

Fluckey prepared for a second attack. He was feeling very aggressive. "The escorts are more scared than we are," he insisted. As *Barb* approached the convoy, a target in its sights, a destroyer suddenly turned and bore down on the sub. Magnified by the sonar loudspeaker, the warship's high power screws whirred menacingly. It was a perfect setup for a "down-the-throat" shot, but *Barb* had not yet reloaded her forward torpedoes. Fluckey felt his aggressiveness vanishing. He ordered a crash dive. *Barb* assumed deep submergence at 140 feet, with only mud below, to wait out the depth charges. Eventually the destroyer went away and *Barb* came up to periscope depth. It required another hour of patient tracking before the sub was in position to fire again. Darkness having fallen, *Barb* surfaced. This second torpedo attack sank one freighter and completely engulfed a second in billowing clouds of smoke. Fluckey called this one a probable, based on the half-size pip on the radar screen.

The convoy was by this time in a state of panic and in complete disarray, which made the subs' task harder. Contrary to what one might suppose, i.e., that a flurried convoy could the more easily be picked off ship by ship, the attacking submarine's problems of tracking and developing a firing setup were magnified. The time it took to get from one victim to the next often consumed half a day or more. The destroyer escorts, however, made sonar contact with *Picuda* and *Queenfish* and dashed off to give chase, enabling *Barb* to slip in for a third attack. Three torpedoes striking an ammunition carrier produced "a stupendous, earth-shaking eruption," which, in Fluckey's estimation, "far surpassed Hollywood, and was one of the biggest explosions of the war."

The effect aboard *Barb* was startling. A high vacuum threatened to suck men in the control room up the hatch.

159

In the conning tower, their shirts were pulled violently over their heads. Fluckey, on the bridge, had the air wrenched out of his lungs, and it was a long moment before he could order the sub "All ahead flank."

As the submarine pulled forward, a cascade of shrapnel began to rain over her superstructure. The horizon was as bright as if lit by daylight, and the target resembled nothing so much as a gigantic phosphorus bomb. Awestruck, Fluckey alternated ducking for cover and gawking at the spectacle. Sweeping with his binoculars, he was able to see only one freighter remaining. The escorts were milling around aimlessly. They no longer had anything to escort.

Fluckey was content at that point to make his departure, but the Engineering Officer, who had never seen a ship sunk, pleaded with him to pursue the surviving cargoman.

"Skipper," the young officer pleaded, "I love to hear the thump, thump, thump of the torpedoes and see millions of bucks go sky high."

At that point, however, *Queenfish* radioed in for a piece of the action and *Picuda* put her bid in also. With a twelve torpedo expenditure, Fluckey had sunk four ships, probably sunk another and damaged a sixth. To the dismay of the Engineering Officer, his skipper agreed that *Barb* had had more than her share. *Barb* headed south into the Formosa Strait. After only nine days at sea, her eleventh war patrol was already an unqualified success, and except for minor damage caused by concussion and shrapnel, and the foul pungency of burnt gunpowder which hung in the air for days afterwards, she was in splendid trim. The crew was in high spirits. They were in hopes that this would turn out to be a record-breaking patrol.

For the next two weeks, however, *Barb* tracked the normal convoy routes without success, sighting nothing larger than a canal barge. Apparently, the convoys were laying low. Or were they? Fluckey had, in addition to a large share of audacity, a restless, inquiring mind. He was sure that things were not what they seemed. He pored over his charts and mulled over the situation.

USAAF raids on Formosa were keeping Japanese merchant shipping bottled up on that island. Traffic had all but ceased, according to reports. Fluckey reasoned that if convoys were running at all—and, clearly, they were, since their cargoes were so badly needed by the home islands—they were plying the inshore route along the China coast. They were not running at night. At any rate, he had not observed any lights. Consequently he concluded that the Japs were running only in the daytime along the new, close coast route where it would be foolhardy if not fatal for a submarine to prowl.

Confirmation by radio came from China-based coast-watchers of Commodore Milton E. Miles' Navgroup China, which also alerted Fluckey to a particular convoy then working its way up the coast. Frustrated by the weeks of inactivity, the restless young skipper determined to press into the shallow coastal waters to flush out the convoy. He realized that it was a job more suited to a PT boat, but he knew that if the targets continued to play coy, there would be no action unless he took daring chances.

Based on Commodore Miles' report, Fluckey assumed the convoy to be anchored at Foochow the night of

January 21. He estimated that a day's run would take the freighter as far northward as Wenchow. Accordingly, he made plans to mingle with the Chinese junk fleet halfway between these two ports, 15 miles off the coastline at Namkwan Harbor. At that point, the sub would be lying inside the 20-fathom curve, barely enough for safe submergence; less than half the amount needed to evade depth charges if they came under attack.

Late in the afternoon of January 22, after several hours of a tense, expectant stakeout, Fluckey's deductions proved correct. Three to six ships were sighted far to the south. Elated, Fluckey began a pursuit. In the next few hours, however, darkness fell and the prey vanished. There were no ships' lights to be seen. They had anchored, very likely, safe in the confines of Namkwan Harbor where no American submarine dared go. There were minefields to contend with, shore batteries, searchlights, escort vessels, and waters marked "Unexplored," "Dangerous Rocks," "Rocks, position doubtful," "Rocks Awash." Worst of all, within the 10-fathom curve, a submarine could not submerge at all.

If *Barb* were to follow the merchant ships into Namkwan, it would mean more than an hour's run on the surface and then, after a torpedo attack, another hour's run, surfaced, with a pack of depth-charging destroyers hard on her heels.

A very dangerous undertaking, Fluckey realized; hardly a mission for a sensible man.

On the other hand, there were factors that would work in *Barb*'s favor. Most important of all was the element of surprise. The enemy wouldn't dream any submarine could be reckless enough to attempt such a raid. There was a good chance radar operators might be less attentive than they ought to be. Also, it was a dark, forbidding night; visibility was very poor, and the sub had a low-slung silhouette that could easily be mistaken for a sampan on a moonless night. Finally, *Barb's* retirement through the offshore junk fleet, where the charts noted rocks, might discourage pursuit.

Fluckey weighed the very real hazards against the dim hope of good luck and made his decision. After careful deliberation, he sat down and wrote in his log: "Fully realize our critical position and the potential dangers involved . . . figure the odds are 10 to 1 . . . in our favor . . . man battle stations, torpedoes!"

Barb began the run in at one A.M., January 23, approaching Namkwan from the south. The black-hulled sub surfaced and crossed the 20-fathom curve southeast of the Piseang Islands, working gradually inshore. The crew was very tense, more tense than Fluckey had ever known them to be. It was so quiet that even the normal sounds of breathing were magnified and became an irritant. The engines throbbed dully. *Barb* turned north. After half an hour of running silent—air conditioners, ventilation system, all unessential machinery turned off —the heat began to build appreciably. The island of Fuyan fell astern. Except for an occasional sounding, "Ten fathoms," "Nine fathoms," "Eight fathoms," nobody felt impelled to speak.

The Torpedo and Gunnery Officer flicked on the Torpedo Data Computer (TDC). The device, into which all pertinent data for a torpedo setup were fed, emitted a low-pitched whine as the motor came up to speed. A quartermaster stood by the firing panel, a metal box with glass windows, red lights glowing, several rows of switches and the firing key, a plunger with brass plate curved to fit the palm of the hand. The quartermaster smiled nervously and flicked imaginery dust from the key. Several men wiped their foreheads with towels.

Shortly after passing Fuyan, *Barb* came abreast of the Incog Islands. Just northwest of these islands lay Nàmkwan Harbor.

"Skipper, we're getting Jap radar interference on the A-scope," a voice called out. "I make out three patrol boats."

"All ahead one third," Fluckey ordered. *Barb* shuddered and slowed, and inched cautiously around the Incog Islands. It was then three A.M. One of the escort warships appeared to be patrolling several thousand yards to the northeast. A second destroyer was farther into the harbor. The third, less than a mile off, was slowly cruising south towards the Incogs. There was a moment of great tension. The lighthouse on one of the small cluster of islands swept a 360-degree arc, but farther out to sea, and the night was very dark. One young sailor stared at the hull with wide eyes as if expecting to see a shell come bursting through. The destroyer passed between the islands and the mainland, disappearing from the radar screen. Several more crewmen wiped themselves with towels.

"He didn't see us," somebody said.

Fluckey nodded. "He seemed more concerned with using his radar to keep himself off the rocks. What are we getting on the screen now?"

"Contact on a large group of anchored ships in the lower reaches of Namkwan," was the reply. Fluckey nodded absently. He could feel his excitement mounting. He had expected perhaps five or six ships. Now it appeared there were many more. Quickly, he set final preparations in motion; these included a complete realignment of the attack team. He secured the bridge and took over the conning tower, moved the assistant approach officer from target plot to navigational plot and put the plotting officer on the Position Plan Indicator (PPI) Scope, an invaluable short-range radar which reproduced objects like ships' hulls as blobs on the screen, making them as apparent as they would be through visual sightings.

Fluckey may have had the same motives for the unorthodox rotation of stations as the skipper who had tried it earlier in the war, explaining to Admiral Charles Lockwood, "I found that if I stayed on the bridge, those ships out there in the dark looked awfully close and I usually got scared and fired at too long range." In any case, Fluckey sent one of the junior officers up to the bridge and handled the attack from the conning tower.

Slowly, *Barb* crept forward. The only sound was the fathometer thumping. "Single ping sounding, 6 fathoms," announced a strained voice.

Fluckey considered ordering the crew to put on life jackets, but one look around the conning tower made him decide otherwise. The terrible strain showed clearly on their faces. They were taut, grey-white. He could see hands trembling. Breathing was shallow, both from the temperature and the high tension. The suggestion that life jackets might be needed would clearly do more harm than good.

It was then 3:25 A.M.

"Skipper," the radarman said hoarsely, "take a look at this scope. It's got the illuminated measles."

The Exec. peered over the seaman's shoulder. "Ships," he said.

Fluckey took a look and shook his head. "Can't be. The Japs don't have that many ships."

"Ships," the first lieutenant insisted. "Ships."

Fluckey could feel his fingertips tingling. He estimated the heading of the anchored ships and the current of the sea. He plotted the navigational position from which the attack would be made. *Barb* continued to creep forward, narrowing the range moment by moment. Apparently, she hadn't yet been spotted. She was then running directly northwest towards the dark, silent harbor. The fathometer thumped and the PPI scope sounded the targets' echoes. Fluckey began counting the blobs. He could see ships banked three deep, in three columns about 500 yards apart, with a few scattered farther inshore.

"I count twelve ships on one bearing," the radar officer broke in excitedly. Fluckey kept counting. By the time he reached thirty, he felt as if his pulse were going to break through his skin.

"This must be the most beautiful target of the war," he marveled. "Even an erratic torpedo can't miss." By actual measurement, the target length was 4,200 yards. The time was then 3:52 A.M. and *Barb* had closed to within 6,000 yards.

"Make ready all tubes," he said, surprised his voice sounded as calm and crisp as it did. He chose one of the large ships in the center of the near column as the primary target. The range and the bearing were marked and the TDC operator fed the data into the complex machine. "Open the outer doors forward," Fluckey ordered. In the forward torpedo room, the torpedomen cranked open the heavy bronze muzzles. This was the last preparatory chore. The "pickles" were in the tube, ready to run. Fluckey took a last look through the scope. The atmosphere in the conning tower was electric. Fluckey took a deep breath. The time was 4:04 A.M. The range was just over 3,000 yards.

"Okay," he said. "It is now time to take one of our well-known calculated risks."

The few smiles that appeared were brief. The tension was too great for much in the way of gallows humour.

"Fire one," Fluckey said.

At the firing panel, the quartermaster flicked the first switch down to a horizontal position and pressed his palm on the key. The first torpedo whooshed out. He flicked the first switch back up again and held his finger poised over the second, waiting for the command.

"Fire two."

Within thirty seconds, four torpedos were on their way, then *Barb* turned briskly about and the stern tubes came around to bear. The fathometer said five fathoms. Chief Gunner's Mate Paul Saunders eyed it ruefully and thought, "We can almost get out and walk." It was a discomfiting thought. Four more torpedoes went out, as the quartermaster flicked his switches and pressed his key with somber concentration. A total of three minutes had elapsed.

"That's it," Fluckey said. "All ahead flank, let's get out of here." As the sub lunged forward, he scrambled up the ladder and through the hatch to the bridge. Peering into the darkness, he waited impatiently for the torpedoes to hit. The second hand of his watch swung around slowly,

167

interminably; it was six minutes after four in the morning, January 23. One second, two seconds more, then *Wham!* the first torpedo struck home. Then a second, and a third. For the next three minutes, Fluckey timed and observed all eight of his pickles striking home as Namkwan Harbor erupted.

Torpedoes number two and three hit a large cargo-man in the first column. Fluckey watched the wounded ship wallow into the water like a great weary beast seeking solace in a mud bath. Torpedo number one slipped past the first column and slammed into an unidentified ship in the second column. After *Barb* made her turn she was blocked from view by the primary target. All that could be seen was a huge plume of smoke curling to the sky. The fourth torpedo hit a large AK (Cargoman) in the third column. The ship burned fiercely, the fire flaring several times before going out suddenly, much in the way it would when a stricken ship settled below the waves. Fluckey called it probably sunk.

There was then a pause of almost a minute before the next volley of pickles struck home. During this time, *Barb* was already high-balling it for the 20-fathom curve, her diesels straining at top flank speed, which was just over 20 knots. She was heading due southeast towards the sleeping junk fleet, where hundreds of unsuspecting Chinese fishermen were shortly to be stunned participants in a hectic chase that might easily have been imagined by Mack Sennett for a movie comedy.

Behind *Barb*, the harbor was a maelstrom, a confusion of rending sounds, acrid odors, billowing flames and turbulent movements. Throughout the harbor, tracers of all sizes flew about in striking red-yellow patterns. It was

168

a scene of unsurpassed beauty and stunning destructiveness. Large calibre projectiles hurled through the air to burst in the water or on other ships. Some of the largest of these even landed ashore. Incendiary shells set more fires, adding to the holocaust. When the second salvo of torpedoes hit, an AE (explosives carrier) was one of the victims. The effect was like the fall of the first in a chain of dominoes—plop, plop, plop. Torpedoes set off hundreds of other projectiles, which landed on other ships, setting more fires, which touched off still more explosives, and so on through the night.

One freighter glowed brighter and brighter in a penumbra of smoke and flame before it exploded. Another large ship, an AE, had no side. The entire length of the hull had been blown out by the blast of her own magazines. This ship sank moments later. Several large projectiles which Fluckey estimated to be 6-to-12-inch shells passed overhead as *Barb* sped out to sea. All over the harbor, searchlights flicked on and began tracking the dark night sky, on the assumption that the damage had been caused by an air raid. Antiaircraft artillery batteries began firing blindly.

By this time, the smoke spewing and gushing from the damaged ships completely obscured the anchorage. No more ships could be seen. *Barb* passed the ten-fathom curve and moved into an area marked "Unexplored" on the charts. Her skipper would have liked to slow up but caution at that moment seemed the less wise choice. From far astern the Japanese destroyers had come to some semblance of order and were beginning to pursue. The warships could make speeds almost twice that of *Barb* and they were armed with heavy calibre deck guns in addition to the deadly depth charges, whereas *Barb* could only muster a 40-mm. deck gun and automatic weapons. As Fluckey had expected, the escorts steamed out in hot pursuit. It wasn't possible to tell how many of them there were but that hardly mattered. If only one of them found *Barb*, the escapade would end badly indeed.

As *Barb* passed through the unexplored waters and came up to the junk fleet, the destroyers were still well astern, but narrowing the gap. Bursting into the middle of the small fishing boats lying to, the submarine began to weave perilously to avoid smashing into them. She was then making 21.6 knots—for the first time in her life —and slipping through narrow passages, veering, maneuvering wildly in a bit of broken field running that would have done credit to the shiftiest of halfbacks. Fluckey expected at any moment to be playing host to a family of startled fishermen camped on the bow.

Many of the people aboard the junks were asleep despite the great to-do, or perhaps they preferred to stay under cover and out of trouble, but some of them popped up to look and stared wide-eyed as the 300-foot-plus submarine barreled past. Nobody cheered, but there did seem to be a lot of pointing and jabbering.

By four-thirty A.M., after running for about twenty minutes, *Barb* had managed to clear the junk fleet. Fluckey could hear sounds of gunfire from well astern, which meant either the escorts had picked the sub up on their radar screens or they were firing blind. The former seemed the more likely. The rounds fell well short, however, and a number of them landed amid the junk fleet. "Some poor junks are getting it," was Fluckey's thought. It would be even worse for the hapless fishermen if the large sub chasers went steaming into their midst. Whether they did or not, Fluckey never knew. At 4:38, a beam of light flicked on at Tae Island to the north, presumably to aid the onrushing warships' navigation, and that was the last sign of pursuit Fluckey saw. *Barb* sped south of Tae Island, then past a sliver of land marked "Strawstack" on the charts. At 4:45, Fluckey sent a contact report to *Picuda*. For the first time, the other subs of the wolf pack found out what the big flap in Namkwan was all about. They had seen the glow on the horizon and wondered.

Twenty-six minutes later, *Barb* crossed the 20-fathom curve, and for the first time in more than two hours, Fluckey was able to breath easily. Now, if necessary, *Barb* could dive. The skipper's legs felt a bit rubbery, but otherwise he was exhilerated, almost mirthful. He secured the bridge and scrambled below.

"The Galloping Ghost of the China Coast crossed the 20-fathom curve with a sigh," he wrote in his log. "Never realized how much water that was before. However, life begins at forty—fathoms. Kept going."

Assuming that the enemy would expect him to submerge, Fluckey elected to stay on the surface when dawn came up. Half an hour later, however, radar picked up a plane at 7 miles, and by the time it had closed to within two and one-half miles, Fluckey decided his wily ruse was a flop. He exercised the skipper's privilege of changing his mind. *Barb* crash dived and stayed submerged until noon.

The crew was roistering with excitement. Everybody had stories to tell, each providing some highly-charged bardic contribution to the saga of *Barb*'s knife-thrust at-

171

tack and madcap getaway. With the danger past, the adventure quickly bubbled over into myth, especially as the crew recalled it. It was the sort of experience destined from the beginning to be legendary—if successful. But there was no gainsaying Gunner's Mate Saunders' description of *Barb*'s dash to safety:

"We got away from Namkwan like a two-year-old at Santa Anita."

Barb wasn't yet done with assaulting the Japanese merchant fleet, however. On January 29, Fluckey made contact with a large freighter and a medium transport escorted by one warship. There was at the time a driving rain squall that buffeted *Barb* and whipped the sea up, but there were four torpedoes still in the tubes so Fluckey shot them off. He always had a lingering feeling of guilt if he returned from patrol with any ammunition unexpended. Two hits were heard, though unobserved, and the freighter disappeared from the radar screen. Since the timing of the torpedo run was at wide variance with the range set, Fluckey claimed no credit, but ComSubPac was a good sport and gave him a "Damaged" on it anyway.

Barb arrived at Midway Island on February 10, after some navigational difficulties which the skipper wryly described in his log. His tone clearly indicated how jubilant he felt about his exceptional patrol. For an official war patrol report, there are strange intimations of high glee and boyish good spirits in the entry:

"February 10. Commenced search for Midway, which had moved northward at 4 knots during the night. 1130 hours. Finally overtook Midway and moored."

Five days later, *Barb* was in Pearl Harbor, eventually making its way to the West Coast for overhaul in a navy yard. Captain and crew dispersed for well-earned shore leaves followed by duty less subject to abrupt termination due to enemy action.

Commander Fluckey, however, was no man to sit idle for any length of time. In due course he paid a visit to Admiral Lockwood at Pearl Harbor. He had a plan, which the admiral at first turned down. *Barb*'s skipper was not to be deterred, however. There were things he wanted to do with a submarine which had not yet been tried. Lockwood's resolution wavered in the face of the younger man's enthusiasm.

It had been the admiral's intention to send *Barb* on a milk run patrol to Wake Island. The submarine had already made four dangerous patrols and, in the submariner's jargon, had used up her "J Factor." In other words, she had expended her supply of luck. Wake Island had long since been bypassed in the island-hopping strategy, and was being used as a bombing practice area for new flyers. Submarines were needed for "Lifeguard" duty there. Prudence dictated sending *Barb*, for her twelfth and last patrol, on this relatively safe assignment.

Fluckey, however, would have none of it. He coaxed and cajoled and finally Admiral Lockwood relented. As a result, *Barb* left Pearl Harbor on June 8 on what was to be, if not the most destructive, then surely one of the most varied and unorthodox submarine patrols of the war.

Fluckey wanted to go north of Hokkaido, in order to seek out the remnants of the Japanese fleet which were thought to be hiding in some out-of-the-way anchorage.

173

He knew the waters well, having patrolled there from May to July of the previous year. There were two bays, one of which could be reached by submarine only after a 60-mile haul on the surface, which he considered good bets, especially since the air force hadn't patrolled there.

A second goal was the harassment of Japanese coastal installations on northern Hokkaido and Karafuto, which was the portion of Sakhalin Island south of the 50th parallel, and which, having been turned over to Russia after the war, no longer has a Japanese identity. (The city of Shikuka, for example, is now known as Poronaysk; Toyohara is Yuzhno Sakhalinsk and Shiritori is Makarov; but the local population presumably still has trouble pronouncing its L's.)

With this harassment mission in mind, Fluckey decided to try out an armament idea he had been toying with intermittently during the previous months. He went to the proper authorities and requested that they ship a rocket launcher to his submarine, complete with a load of rockets sufficient to bedevil a number of Japanese installations. The response from the Navy was icy. As the winner of a Medal of Honor and three Navy Crosses, Fluckey was no man to be taken idly, but clearly his request for a rocket launcher was nothing short of whimsical. Submarines did not carry rocket launchers.

"True," Fluckey acknowledged. "That's why I want you to give me one."

"The Navy" was more difficult to deal with and less responsive than any of the individuals who constituted it, but Fluckey did finally manage to make his point. He unrolled a set of charts and indicated a Japanese cable station on one of the southern Kurile Islands. He asked the Navy how much they estimated it was worth. Four million dollars, they replied.

"Fine," Fluckey said. "Give me the rocket launcher and I'll promise you one million dollars worth of damage on that cable station."

This pragmatic, businesslike offer finally convinced the authorities that the persuasive young officer was not chasing fantasies, and the rocket launcher, removed from a beached landing vessel, was delivered to *Barb*.

"Ten minutes before sailing," Fluckey recalled, "they dumped the launcher and 100 rockets aboard." There was some suspicion that a lingering resistance to the idea might have arranged the scheduling. "Furthermore, there were no instructions. No drawings. We even had to figure out the electrical hookups. About all we knew for sure was that you put the rocket into the launcher."

Undismayed, *Barb*'s crew proceeded to remove one of the deck guns and replace it with the rocket launcher. No sooner had the weapon been bolted into place than another problem arose. The rockets were fired electrically. Was there a possibility, Fluckey wondered, that they might not just blow the submarine up when a radio call was made? After much discussion, the skipper and his electronics experts came to a conclusion:

"We weren't sure."

Time was pressing, however, and Fluckey was anxious to get going, so as a compromise security measure, the rockets and the radios were separated as far as possible. This seemed to work. At any rate, no accidents occurred during the patrol.

Shortly before departing, Fluckey was notified that the Navy had changed its mind. The Japanese cable sta-

Holding the *Barb*'s battle flag are, left to right, Paul G. Saunders, Billy R. Hatfield, Francis M. Sever, Lawrence Newland, Edward Klinglesmith, James E. Richard, John Markuson, and William M. Walker.

tion wasn't worth anywhere near four million, they decided, and asked for the launcher back. By then it was too late, however. Fluckey had it bolted to his hull and was preparing to cast off, and wasn't about to relinquish his prize. Having no alternative, the Navy let him go. They grudgingly told him to forget about the cable station altogether and use the rockets up on targets of opportunity. That was fine with Fluckey. It was exactly what he had intended all along.

Barb departed Pearl Harbor on June 8, arriving at Midway four days later. During this layover, Fluckey organized a Special Weapons team out of his demolitions squad and proceeded to train them in commando and espionage work, with the intention of using them primarily as a boarding party to heist charts and other valuables from sinking enemy ships.

The training course was necessarily short and rather superficial. The team was by no means expert, as they subsequently proved, but they were eager, they had young adventurous spirits, and they could do a pretty good job when the pressure was on. They proved that also. Among other things, their training included safe-cracking with a shaped charge of plastic TNT which Fluckey called the "Velveeta cheese loaf." The members of this team, led by Lieutenant William Walker, an affable, not very warlike, dark-haired youngster, soon became the envy of the rest of the crew. All of them, at one time or another, were offered large sums of money to relinquish a place on the team, but all refused. Special Weapons promised to be a lark.

Barb limbered up for the more difficult work to follow by attacking and sinking a pair of luggers off Kunashiki. Early the following morning, 2:30 A.M. of June 23, rockets were fired from the deck of a submarine for the first time in history. The target was the industrial town of Shari on the north coast of Hokkaido, with a population of 20,000. Some fires were set but it was impossible to appraise the damage with any accuracy.

Just before dawn on the twenty-third, *Barb* engaged in a gun duel with an armed trawler, with the double purpose of taking a prisoner and giving the boarding team some practice. The battle lasted less than half an hour, at the end of which time the trawler was foundering but refused to sink. A number of men forward on the burning trawler had not surrendered, so Fluckey decided not to use his commandos, much to their chagrin. Instead, he sank the ship by making a high speed sweep close aboard. This aggressive maneuver washed a great

177

deal of water into a hole near the waterline—previously opened by the 5-inch gun—and soon the trawler went bubbling to the bottom, sunk with a lighthearted disregard for orthodoxy and a respect for the price of shells rarely found in the combat zone.

The water was full of swimming men, some of whom seemed sincerely not to want to be picked up—one man did himself in by slitting his throat with a knife— and others of whom seemed entirely willing. Only one of these was hauled aboard. His name, it turned out, was Kamikawa, and he was not Japanese but Korean. At one point in his entirely involuntary military career, he had been a gunner on an armed merchantman, and had seen a Japanese soldier slice a Chinese worker's hands off. This had sickened him and confirmed his already strong impression that war was not his game.

Kamikawa, nicknamed Kamikaze by the crew, spoke almost no English, but he was friendly and eager to help in any way possible. He had a great deal of information at his disposal that proved extremely valuable, and he imparted it in torrents of Japanese, gusts of German and broken English and a typhoon of gestures. His familiarity with the local waters proved a great help to navigation and his knowledge of coastal guard procedures later aided the guerrillas when they landed to blow up a train. Kamikaze very shortly was accepted as an honorary member of the crew and moved about with relative impunity.

For a week, *Barb* prowled through La Perouse Strait, along the north coast of Hokkaido and the east coast of Karafuto, making no contacts. Then, on the twenty-ninth, Fluckey stumbled by sheer chance on a small con-

178

voy escorted by five warships. One of these, a *Terutsuki* class destroyer, nearly put an end to the patrol. Fluckey was on the surface and had closed to within 12,000 yards when the man-o'-war opened fire. Not only was the torpedo attack deflected, but the Japanese skipper turned out to be a dogged and talented sub-chaser. For several days, the *Terutsuki* pursued *Barb* with singleminded determination, dropping depth charges until it seemed one must surely cave in the sub's hull. Kamikaze was then not entirely sure he had chosen wisely in joining the U.S. Navy, but he endured the frightening assault stoically.

When finally the last sonar ping faded away and *Barb* made her escape to deeper and safer waters, Fluckey wasted no time getting on with the harassment missions. He chose as his target the island of Kaihyo To. Perhaps because of the extended drubbing *Barb* had taken, Fluckey felt that more than a token bombardment was called for. Once again he was feeling aggressive. He assembled the Special Weapons team and briskly told them they would have the honor of being the first submariners of the war to assault and capture a Japanese island.

The guerrillas were enthralled. When the news spread, they were the center of attention and the excitement generated soon took on startling proportions. Sailors pleaded with tears in their eyes to be allowed to go along. One man offered $200 for a billet on the team, but he was turned down flat.

The island, rechristened "Little Iwo" for the gala occasion, was in Patience Bay off the east coast of Karafuto. A reconnaissance on July 1 showed 40-mm., 20-mm., and 5-inch gun emplacements on the cliffs. Of military value on the island were a sealing station, a number of warehouses and barracks buildings, two beacons, a radio antenna and an observation post, all of these on the flat top of the island. At 6:51 A.M., July 2, Fluckey began the bombardment from 1,000 yards out, while the eight men of Special Weapons waited patiently below for their moment of glory. The cliffside emplacements returned the submarine's fire, but with less effect. While no shells hit *Barb*, her own deck guns blew a 75-mm. field piece high into the air, silenced a machine gun, started many fires burning, destroyed the observation post and 20 or more of the buildings and torched an oil dump.

By 11 A.M., the guerrillas were topside preparing to debark into small boats when, at the last minute, a number of concrete pillboxes previously silent began to speak. This put a new complexion on things. The commandos were no longer enchanted by the prospect of being the first members of a submarine crew ever to capture a Japanese island. "You can buy me for a nickel," one of them suggested to a shipmate, who promptly shook his head. The rate of exchange could hardly have been bettered, but nobody came forward. Since the fire from the pillboxes would certainly have made a hash of the raid, Fluckey canceled it, and contented himself instead with pumping some rounds at the emplacements, with minimal success. He did have the satisfaction, however, of seeing one lucky round from the 40-mm. deck gun go into the slit of a pillbox and blow off the front side.

The Assault Team went below to brood.

For the next two weeks, *Barb* carried out a miscellany of missions, including a second rocket assault, on Shikuka in Patience Bay, and the sinking of a coastal

180

freighter. From July 12–15, *Barb* engaged in lifeguard duties for air strikes on northern Hokkaido. The attacking planes came from carriers of Admiral Halsey's 7th Fleet. Listening in on their chatter, Fluckey was treated to the following interchange during the height of the bombardment:

Pilot to section leader: "There's a horse, I'm going after him."

Section leader to pilot: "You leave that poor horse alone."

On the nineteenth, Fluckey finally decided the time had come to unleash his Assault Team, which had been fretting with inactivity. In addition to all the other things a submarine crew had never done, none had ever blown up a train, a concept that appealed to Fluckey's sense of daring and perhaps his sense of humor. It was Fluckey's fond hope that *Barb*'s guerrillas would remedy the oversight. Accordingly, with his characteristic bounding enthusiasm, he made plans to land the saboteurs on Karafuto with a 55-pound demolition charge.

The general plan was to blow up a train at some vital point on the east coast rail system which, though narrow gauge, was used by engines of the larger, European type. Trains ran from 7 to 32 cars. After extensive offshore reconnaissance, Fluckey had the rail timetable accurately charted and had selected a site where three lines merged and then diverged again, thus guaranteeing a maximum tie-up of rails. The landing would be made on a lonely stretch of beach 700 yards distant from the nearest houses. There the submarine could approach to within 1,000 yards offshore without grounding.

By the following night, all details had been checked and rechecked. The saboteurs were ready to land, but a very bright near-full moon induced a cancellation. The following night was also, in Fluckey's words, "another lovers' night."

The raiding party was at a fever pitch of readiness, but Fluckey counseled patience, and by noon of the twenty-second, southerly breezes sprang up, bringing with them a cloud front sufficient to mask the espionage operations. Fluckey passed the word along that the commandos would land that night.

"After days of patiently waiting and observing, the undercurrent of expected action that ran through the boat made one's spine tingle," Fluckey recalled. Even the prisoner, Kamikaze, uncharacteristically felt a call to arms. After giving extensive data on the dog patrols that guarded the coastline, he volunteered to join the party. Popular sentiment aboard the boat favored Kamikaze's cause, and he did enjoy a good deal of trust, but the skipper felt it would be needlessly endangering the saboteurs' safety, and accordingly, vetoed the Korean's application.

At 10 P.M., *Barb* surfaced, flooded down, and under the protective mantle of the low-hanging overcast, approached the beach on batteries. Topside a large number of crewmen had gathered to inflate the two rubber boats, to help in loading the equipment and to increase their own sense of participation. Many of them had a difficult time controlling their envy, as evidenced by the ceaseless twitting of the landing party, which consisted of Lieutenant William Walker, SM 2/C Francis Sever, MoMM 2/C James Richard, MoMM 1/C John Markuson, CGM Paul Saunders, EM 3/C Billy Hatfield, SC 1/C Lawrence Newland and TM 3/C Edward Klinglesmith.

Fluckey gave these men a final briefing and ran through the communications plan, which was strong on avian effects: the signal for an alert was two bobwhite whistles; for assembly, whippoorwill whistles; for an emergency dash to the boats, a mechanical whistle. The bird whistles, incidentally, came from a fund of Boy Scout memories which Fluckey shared with some of the crew. There were also signals for communicating with the submarine: a "W" on the blinker gun indicated the landing party was returning to *Barb*, one Very star at 15-minute intervals meant "We are unable to locate the submarine after 30 minutes paddling from the beach;" two Very stars, "We are in trouble, lay a barrage in the direction indicated." One Very star from *Barb* meant "We are in trouble, will return every night."

After half an hour of running slowly in towards the shore, everything seemed to be going perfectly. The weather was ideal, the sea calm and the tide slack. Then word came topside that the SJ radar had picked up two small ships at 4,500 yards, probably luggers, but possibly small patrol boats, coming down the coast.

"Man battle stations, guns," Fluckey ordered. All landing preparations came to a halt and with baited breath, crewmen stood by their guns as the boats passed by. For many long moments, there was a complete absence of motion and a charged silence as the Japanese boats chugged slowly past the bow. Evidently they hadn't spotted the submarine, or if they had, had failed to identify it. Soon the luggers disappeared into the night.

183

Barb's crewmen sprang back into action, loading the equipment onto the rubber boats. In addition to the 55 pounds of MK 108 demolitions and the electrical equipment, the boats carried carbines, tommy guns, hand grenades, home manufactured shovels and picks, a blinker gun, a Very signal pistol, binoculars, line and wedges.

By midnight, *Barb* was in position some 950 yards offshore, with only two fathoms under her keel. The rubber boats were launched. The eight men of the assault team stepped into the boats, each man equipped with a red flashlight, a watch, a knife, two "D" rations, a lifejacket, a cigarette lighter and a pistol. As the boats shoved off, the skipper leaned towards them to send them on their way with some appropriate phrase.

Intending to be briskly professional, Fluckey instead found himself overcome with excitement, his mind a blank. At the last moment, he did manage to say, "Boys, if you get stuck head for Siberia 130 miles north." Not at all the hearty send-off he had intended. The Assault Team paddled off.

The sabotage raid was then completely out of Fluckey's hands. All he could do was stand on the bridge and watch the coastline for signs of failure or success. He might have felt even more trepidation than he did had he been along with the commandos on the comedy of errors that ensued.

The submarine, first of all, had navigated to some 500 yards north of the assigned landing beach, despite having used radar; then, the saboteurs, paddling slowly in to shore through the haze, lost sight of the two prominent peaks that were to have been their markers; and, furthermore, the boat compasses were erratic. As a result, the saboteurs landed half an hour after midnight in a Japanese backyard, not 50 yards from a house, which fortunately was dark, its occupants asleep. There were dog tracks and human footprints on the beach, so Lieutenant Walker with understandable caution ordered a preliminary reconnaissance, which came back to report that they had, in fact, landed in the middle of a Japanese village. No dogs barked, however, and there was no sign of life, so Walker decided they could continue the mission without undue apprehension. The signalman, Francis Sever and Guard Lawrence Newland stayed behind to watch the boats while the other six men proceeded inshore, prudently skirting the houses.

What had appeared from the submarine to be short grass turned out instead to be waist-high bullrushes, which snapped underfoot. As the six crouched saboteurs pussyfooted through it, there arose a hideously noisy crunch and crackle with every foot fall.

Crunch. Crunch. (Pause) Snap. (Pause) Crunch. On top of this, everybody took to hissing, "Sshh! Sshh!" Walker began saying "Sshh" to stop the others from saying "Sshhh," and amid a spiraling panic, they sped onward hissing like reptiles and convinced that the Japanese High Command in Tokyo had already been notified of their presence.

To make things worse, the several members of the team developed a tendency to travel at their own speeds, with predictable results. They met each other at intervals, as fearful agents from alien worlds: a dark shape, breath caught in the throat, heart misfiring, trigger-finger and weapon poised; and, following the recognition, an exchange of taut mutterings. This scene, repeated a

185

dozen times ("Don't you know you almost got your dumb damned head blown off?") quickly threatened to drive Walker mad with grief.

After what seemed an eternity, they finally cleared the bullrushes and came to a highway, where they paused to mop their foreheads. Walker again sent guards out north and south, both of whom reported all clear. Somewhat heartened by this interim sign of success, Walker instructed them to get across the road singly and as quickly as possible. In the best Marine Corps tradition, he said tensely, "Follow me," jumped up and fell headlong into a four-foot ditch. Unhurt, but with his dignity somewhat ruffled, he scrambled up and said "Watch out for that ditch there." In the darkness, the men cleared their throats and nodded soberly. Not at all nonplussed, the young officer once again said "Follow me," and dashed quickly across the highway. On the other side was another four-foot ditch which, unfortunately, he had not entirely anticipated, and once again the high-flying Walker fell headlong to earth, a minor Icarus. The others all made it across the road without incident, and from that moment on, Walker eschewed the grand gesture. One hundred yards farther on, they came to the tracks. After a short reconnaissance, Walker selected his spot. He sent three men, Markuson, Richard and Klinglesmith, out as guards 50 yards north and south and 20 yards inland. Walker, noticing a peculiarly shaped object about 70 yards down the track, instructed Markuson to check on it.

With the guards posted, Gunner's Mate Saunders and Electrician's Mate Hatfield—who was, incidentally, a member of the Hatfield clan of Kentucky which had feuded so many years with the McCoys—began digging under the track with the homemade picks and shovels, and immediately discovered they would not do. For one thing, they tended to break easily, which left Saunders and Hatfield cursing futilely at the splintered handles. For another, the sound of metal striking rang out like a clarion call in the still night. Walker urged them to make less noise. They very gladly put down the tools, and just at that moment the sounds of running and scuffling echoed from the south. They could see a dark shape dashing towards them. In a panic, Walker, Saunders and Hatfield dove for cover and trained their weapons on the advancing form, which sounded as if it was saying "Lookout tower, lookout tower."

It turned out to be Markuson, breathing heavily, and in a highly agitated state. He squatted down beside them. Walker informed him he had almost been shot.

"You're supposed to give the bobwhite whistle to sound the alert," Walker said angrily. "Why didn't you whistle?"

"I tried to whistle," Markuson replied indignantly, "but when I saw that tower my mouth dried up."

The four men sat motionless for several minutes and, as it was apparent that the tower wasn't occupied, Markuson soon went back to his post. The other three men commenced digging, this time with their bare hands. The earth wasn't particularly soft. They all broke fingernails. But it was preferable to serenading the countryside with the sound of picks and shovels. After a very few minutes, they noticed a light flickering a long way down the track.

"Now what?" Walker asked crossly. They stopped working to watch the light, which soon disappeared.

"Maybe it's a train," Saunders suggested, though none

was scheduled. They all put their ears to the ground, listening intently. While they were thus occupied, a long, blacked-out freight train came roaring around a curve less than 100 yards away. In horror, the saboteurs lunged for cover.

There wasn't very much in the way of concealment close at hand. There were a few bushes some six inches high and two inches wide. Walker and Saunders tried to make do with these, but felt inordinately exposed. Hatfield threw himself flat on the ground. There was a loud retort that sounded very much like a rifle burst.

"I'm shot," Hatfield moaned and rolled over. Walker and Saunders ran to his side. "I'm shot," Hatfield repeated. Walker and Saunders stared down at him with eyes widening, as Hatfield began to expand about the middle.

All this time, the train was barreling past them, and the engineer was leaning far out of his cab with a puzzled look on his face, giving them a somber appraisal. None of them had enough élan to wave a greeting, but they all assumed what they hoped were innocent-looking postures.

By the time the train had flashed by, Hatfield was sitting up and comprehension was lightening his face. He had, on making contact with the ground, somehow managed to set off the carbon dioxide cartridges that inflated the lifebelt. Sheepishly, he stood up.

"You're not shot," Saunders said, "You're pregnant."
Walker urged them back to work.

After only a bit more scrabbling in the dirt, the charge was placed in the hole along with the battery, and the firing circuits were tested and adjusted. While Hatfield made the final hookups, Walker pursed his lips and did his best to imitate a whippoorwill. Saunders joined in and soon the night was filled with trilling bird calls, a pastoral note in the midst of wartime skullduggery. (Whippoorwills, incidentally, are not native to Karafuto, but it seemed likely no ornithologist would be close enough at hand to endanger the enterprise.)

The guards came running up, Hatfield covered the hole to disguise the digging and the team prepared to depart. At this point, Hatfield, who had once worked on a railroad back in Kentucky, decided that Fluckey had misgauged the pressure switch clearance; that is, miscalculated the amount of pressure required to depress the micro switch sufficiently to activate the charge. He bent down and began tapping the pressure switch. Everybody else blanched. If Hatfield had tapped the switch a millimeter too far, the charge would have blown up in their faces, as they were well aware. He was very sure of himself, however, and argued that it would have been a terrible shame if they had gone to all that trouble and failed because too much tolerance had been set into the switch.

Hatfield continued to tap the switch gently, with infinite care, until finally the white-faced Walker ordered him to cease and desist.

"I don't care how far off the Old Man is," Walker said grimly. "Don't do that again."

Since Walker had the full support of the others, Hatfield didn't press the issue, though he seemed a bit hurt at having his expertise challenged. The party traced their steps back to the beach. On the way, Walker handled the roadside ditches with great aplomb, and even the snapping and crunching and crackling of the bullrushes fazed no one. The ease with which the mission had, so far, been carried out, made them infinitely less susceptible to fear. Some of them, in fact, became positively coltish and light-headed, so much so that, on passing through the Japanese village, they suggested giving battle with hand grenades. They very much wanted to toss a few of them into bedroom windows. Walker nixed this very firmly, and—after only a short argument—managed to herd them down to the beach without further incident.

The launching of the rubber boats turned out to be more difficult than anticipated. It was only after considerable struggling that the eight men, now thoroughly soaked, managed to start paddling away from the shore. The boats were equipped with radar corners, by which means they could be tracked from the submarine, and at 1:32 A.M. the message was flashed topside that the boats were leaving the beach. Muffled cheers greeted this report. The boats began sending the "W" message by blinker gun.

At 1:45, the submariners lining the deck to observe the results of the raid heard a northbound train coming down the tracks. Fluckey, galvanized by the great moment, was afraid the blast might damage the men in the boats. He broke silence to yell at them, "Paddle like the devil!" which was entirely unnecessary. The commandos, having themselves spotted the train, began "churning like egg beaters." The train rounded the bend, rapidly approaching the planted charge. The commandos stopped paddling to look. Flushed with anticipation, the submariners held their breaths, staring intently at the dim outlines of the onrushing train. At 1:47, the locomotive depressed the micro switch.

190

"WHAM!" Fluckey recorded. "What a thrill! What a beautiful sight!"

The engine boilers blew up. There was a bright flash and billowing clouds of smoke and through it flew large hunks of steel and wood 200 feet in the air. "Cars piled up and rolled off the track in a writhing, twisting, mass of wreckage," Fluckey wrote in his log. "Cheers!"

The mission had been an unqualified success, despite the amateurish execution which threatened it at every step, and the commandos, hauled aboard wet and shivering were feted and lauded over a libation of "medicinal" alcohol. Walker was promptly nicknamed "Choo-Choo," and Fluckey admitted to feeling prouder than he would have been at sinking "a hundred ships."

The guerrilla raid was the high point but by no means the final adventure of the last, unorthodox patrol of the roistering *Barb*. On July 24, there was a rocket assault on Shiritori and, several hours later, another on Kashiho. In the middle of the following afternoon, Lieutenant (j.g.) King led a boarding party onto a burning sampan, captured three anchors and a steering wheel and took one prisoner who informed them that the local Japanese newspapers had credited the train wreck to an air raid. The saboteurs were rather miffed to hear it.

All the rockets having been expended at this point, Fluckey disposed of his remaining forty-three 5-inch shells on a bombardment of Chiri which destroyed a cannery. With all his large calibre ammunition gone, he knew that he would be ordered to return to base, so he put *Barb* on radio silence and made excuses to continue cruising. At Shibetoro, on the west coast of Kunashiri Island, he found a lumber mill and a shipyard in which a large number of sampans were being built. The sub-

191

marine's 40-mm. shells set many fires which razed the area, burning down the lumber mill and most of the sampans, bringing *Barb's* score of these small vessels to 38 for the patrol.

Fluckey had a bet on with his first lieutenant, Lieutenant Commander James Webster, that *Barb* would sink 15 ships on that patrol and, while none of the beached sampans counted, the total of trawlers and luggers and coastal freighters to that point was 14. With no large calibre ammunition left, Fluckey had just about reconciled himself to losing the bet when, late that afternoon, a trawler crossed *Barb's* path. Fluckey assaulted it with rifle grenades, 20-mm. shells and .30- and .50-calibre machine guns, mortally wounding the ship. However, it refused to sink, and Webster stubbornly refused to count it unless he personally saw it sink beneath the waves. Galled, Fluckey ordered *Barb* to ram her. Webster, of course, was furious. He thought this was very bad form. However, the submarine nudged the trawler, her side caved in and soon she sank stern first with her foremast snapping across the bow.

"I win the bet," Fluckey gloated. Webster was surly about it but he conceded defeat, and when *Barb* reached Midway, presented his skipper with "32 ounces of the finest Midway had to offer."

Thus ended the wartime career of the *Barb*, which afterwards was turned over to the Italian Navy to be rechristened *Enrique Tazzoli*; the only submarine of the war to sink an enemy vessel with a wave from her bow, or with a gentle nudge from this same secret weapon; the only one to blow up a train, destroy a cannery, demolish a seal rookery. Of her exploits on this final war patrol, the only one not touched by whimsey was her use of rockets. Subsequently, after Fluckey had proved its worth, a launcher was placed on five more submarines, with an additional dozen in the works at war's end. It was intended that the Silent Service would take over all the Northern Fleet's shore bombardment missions. The subsequent development of missile-carrying undersea boats can be traced back to these crude beginnings.

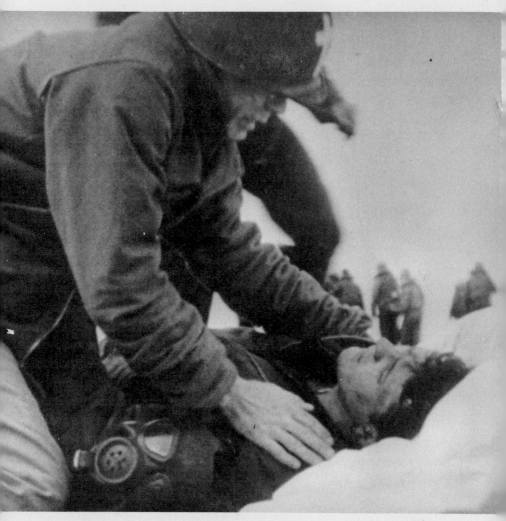
Chaplain Joseph O'Callahan ministering to a wounded sailor aboard the U.S.S. *Franklin*

7

THE PADRE'S
BLACK DAY

〰〰〰〰〰〰〰〰〰〰〰〰〰〰〰〰〰〰〰〰〰〰〰〰

CHAPLAIN JOSEPH TIMOTHY O'CALLAHAN

U.S.S. Franklin

MARCH 19, 1945

As the war in the Pacific entered its fourth year, the exhaustion of the Japanese capacity to resist what had already become an inevitable end was such that, by March of 1945, Admiral Marc Mitscher's Task Force 58 could steam with relative impunity to within 100 miles of the Japanese home islands, there to launch raids on factories, air bases, supply ports and military installations of Honshu and Kyushu. The Japanese fleet no longer ventured forth to give battle; it had been, since the decisive Battle for Leyte Gulf, no threat as a striking force.

Defense against the carrier-based air raids was restricted to *Kamikaze* attacks, in which more than half the surviving Japanese pilots were involved, and in which some 5,000 perished. The *Kamikaze*, or Divine Wind, is, in Japanese history, reputed to have twice wrecked the invasion forces of Kublai Khan in the thirteenth century.

The twentieth century equivalent—a Zero carrying a 550-pound bomb—proved less successful, as did the refinements produced by Japanese technology in the last months of the war, such as the *Oka* (Cherry Blossom), the *Kikka* (Mandarin Orange Blossom), the *Baika* (Plum Blossom), and the *Shinyru* (Divine Dragon) which was a glider utilizing rockets for takeoff propulsion. The *Oka*, a flying bomb with a 2,600-pound warhead, could sink a capital ship, and was used with telling effect during the Okinawa campaign that commenced on April 1; though whenever employed, the suicide craft generally had a difficult time getting past the Hellcat screen, and more often than not exploded harmlessly. The American mind, altogether repelled by the concept, nicknamed the *Oka* the *Baka*, which means idiot.

In addition to these one-way vehicles, Japan still had a number of planes flown by pilots who had every intention of returning to their bases. The most powerful of these units was the Imperial Navy's 343rd Air Corps, commanded by Captain Minoru Genda, a brilliant young flyer who had helped develop the shallow-draft torpedoes that made the Pearl Harbor attack so effective. Genda's fighter pilots flew the new *Shiden* (code-named George by the U.S.), heavily armored and capable of speeds in excess of 400 m.p.h. George proved a worthy successor to Zeke. Genda's bomber pilots flew the Aichi D4Y dive bomber, code-named Judy. On March 19, 1945, one of these Judys managed to evade the combat air patrol of Mitscher's task force, and planted two bombs on the flight deck of aircraft carrier *Franklin*. The Judy was shot down moments later, but the damage had been done, and it was far beyond the Japanese pilot's wildest dream of glory. *Franklin* was in for an unparalleled ordeal by fire. Of a complement of more than 3,000 men, 724 were killed and 265 wounded. The worst disaster in American naval history (save for the subsequent sinking of cruiser *Indianapolis*), it would have been worse still had not untold numbers of brave men struggled throughout a day of torment to save the ship. Not all the heroism could possibly have been catalogued, but two men won Medals of Honor, and there were also 19 awards of the Navy Cross, 22 Silver Stars, 115 Bronze Stars and 234 Letters of Commendation.

One of the Medal of Honor recipients was one of the carrier's two chaplains, a Jesuit mathematician and philosopher who had long since acquired his sea legs. A slight, dark-haired, bushy-browed man, Father Joseph Timothy O'Callahan held the rank of Lieutenant Commander in the Chaplain Corps; his unlined face, set off by a pair of prissy rimless eyeglasses, made him appear younger than his years and altogether too cloister-bound for the firing line. He was born in Boston, Massachusetts —a fact that was verified whenever he spoke—on May 14, 1905, and was the possessor of a hearty, down-to-earth, colloquial manner that endeared him especially to the enlisted men. He played poker with them, drank beer with them, and composed songs for the band, which was led by Seaman "Saxy" Dowell, author of "Three Little Fishes" (in an itty-bitty poo) and formerly a sideman with the Hal Kemp band. O'Callahan was exceedingly proud of his cameraderie with the ranks. It protected him from being labeled stuffy, always a danger to a man with a satchelful of academic degrees.

The Padre had a Bachelor of Arts from St. Andrews

197

College in Poughkeepsie, a Master of Arts, a Licentiate of Philosophy, a Bachelor of Sacred Theology and a Licentiate of Sacred Theology, all from Weston College, Weston, Massachusetts. He had been, for two years from 1938 to 1940, Head of the Mathematics Department of Holy Cross. As an Orders man (Society of Jesus), it was necessary for him to get a special dispensation to serve in the armed forces, and he was among the first to request it and receive it. He entered the Chaplain Corps of the U.S. Naval Reserve on August 7, 1940, and three months later, was called to active duty. He served tours at the Naval Air Station, Pensacola; aboard the carrier *Ranger*; at the Naval Air Station, Ford Island, Hawaii; and aboard the carrier *Franklin*. It was aboard *Ranger* that O'Callahan, a life-long landlubber, learned to think of himself as a Navy man, and to relish the traditions of the sea, and to spice his conversation with Navy lingo; he was, in fact, hooked. He came to love the carrier with the special affection sea-going men feel towards their first ships, and to chafe when landlocked. His orders assigning him to *Franklin*, after three months of what he considered relatively inconsequential duties at Ford Island, advised him to proceed immediately and without delay, and this he did gladly, on March 2, 1945.

Aboard *Franklin*, he quickly established the reputation of being a "good guy," and one who sustained his own modest ecumenical movement by engaging his Protestant and Jewish friends in jovial, if slightly self-conscious, religious bantering. The enforced intimacy of service life had a liberating effect on him. Such conversations, he felt, could not have been undertaken in a civilian world where religious and class provincialisms created island enclaves with little, if any, overlap; in the Navy, he said, "there is a cameraderie and an understanding which civilians do not share." He was most pleased, perhaps, by the nickname given him by Doctor Sam Sherman, surgeon for *Franklin*'s Air Group 5. Sherman, an old friend, called him "Rabbi Tim," a title which O'Callahan cherished for much the same reason he liked to be known as an Enlisted Man's Padre. Both of these identities seemed to take him farther from the parochial, humorless seminary-academy life and closer to the sometimes irreverent but more human realities of a world at war.

Franklin sailed from Pearl Harbor to Ulithi, and from there, on March fifteenth, as part of Mitscher's Task Force 58, to "strike the home islands of the Japanese Empire for the first time," as Captain Leslie Gehres, *Franklin*'s skipper, dramatically announced via the public address system as the carrier steamed out of Ulithi harbor. The task force of more than 100 ships, including 16 carriers and 8 battleships, was spread out across more than 50 miles of sea, and above it roared hundreds of Hellcats and Corsairs; a mighty armada which inspired awe and an overpowering confidence in the men who composed it. Yet, though the task force itself was invulnerable, its individual ships were not. At 7:03 A.M. on the morning of March nineteenth, the aircraft carrier *Hancock* radioed to *Franklin*, "Enemy plane closing on you from ahead."

On the bridge, Captain Gehres immediately called the Combat Information Center (CIC) and asked them what they had on their bank of radar screens. CIC sent back a negative report: "Radar Plot to Bridge—screen shows no bogey." *Hancock* had sighted the Judy visually, just before it ducked into a cloud formation some 2,000 feet up and 1,000 feet in front of *Franklin*, whose radar showed blank. Neither did any other ships in the large formation pick up the enemy bomber.

The four carriers of Task Group 58.2, *Franklin*, *Hancock*, *Bataan* and *San Jacinto*, were just then in the middle of launching the first heavy air strike of the day. The target that morning was to be the shipping in Kobe harbor. At 6:45, *Franklin* had turned northeast into the wind and come up to 24 knots. On the hangar deck, Lieutenant Fred Stalcup and his maintenance crews fueled and armed the fighters and bombers. The ready planes taxied to the elevators (*Franklin* had three) which rose ponderously like huge waiters' trays to lock in place and form a portion of the carrier's flight deck. There, the Flight Deck Officer, Lieutenant Fred Harris, began winding them up for the launch with his paddle.

Nine SB2C Helldivers and eight F6F Hellcats had already been launched, and Harris was just in the process of releasing another Helldiver, when the Judy flashed out of the cloud bank and swept over the carrier's deck. Immediately, the forward 5-inch guns and some 40-mm. Bofors took the bomber under fire. Commander E.B. Parker, leader of Air Group 5, who was already in the air, dipped his wings and came down on the Judy, but he was not able to close her before she dropped two 500-pound AP (armor-piercing) bombs. One landed forward, pierced through to the hangar deck and then exploded. The second landed aft, shot past the flight deck, the gallery deck and the hangar deck, and burst amid the wardroom spaces, near the Chief Petty Officers' quarters.

Normally, a vessel the size of *Franklin*, an *Essex*-class carrier displacing 27,000 tons, could have weathered the hits. But circumstances were such that she was, at that moment, doomed to be the agent of her own destruction. On the hangar deck, a vast enclosure running the length of the ship, were 5 bombers, 14 torpeckers and 12 fighters, all of which had been armed and gassed, and which were turning over their propellers. The air reeked of gasoline fumes. When the AP shell exploded, a sheet of flame raced along the length of the deck, igniting the planes. Strewn about the deck were bombs already armed and waiting to be loaded onto the Helldivers and Hellcats and Avengers. The flames touched off these bombs, and within seconds, the hangar deck, and the gallery deck above it, were rocked by explosions and engulfed in flames.

There were, at the time, several hundred men working on the planes; also on the hangar deck, perhaps a hundred more were waiting patiently for breakfast. Above them, on the gallery deck, worked several hundred more men. Very few of these escaped. A few managed to jump over the side. A very few others survived the blasts. One, Lieutenant W.A. Simon, was the only man in CIC (on the gallery deck) wearing a helmet. He was lifted and smashed against the deck *above*, and the helmet saved his skull. The gallery deck workshops were flaming tombs. The Air Group's ready room, where off-duty pilots gathered to relax and chew the fat, was a furnace.

Franklin carried, in all, some 40,000 gallons of high-octane aviation gas. The planes were loaded with almost

30 tons of high explosives, and in lockers and ready magazines there were perhaps 70 more tons of 20-and 40-mm. ammunition, 5-inch shells, bombs of all sorts, and rockets, which were affectionately known as Tiny Tims, and were by far the most destructive weapon in *Franklin's* arsenal. During the first moments after the enemy bombs struck, Commander Henry Hale, the Air Officer, could be heard repeatedly crying, "Jettison the planes with the Tiny Tims first, get the Tiny Tims over the side." Then one of many blasts severed power lines and the speaker went dead. Soon clouds of smoke came gushing up from the ship's interior. *Franklin*, a floating ammo dump, was beginning to blow herself to bits.

When the Judy was first sighted at 7:03, Father O'Callahan and several other officers were sitting in the officers' wardroom on the second deck forward, eating breakfast, which that morning featured French toast. (There was a good deal of griping. French toast, otherwise mockingly called fried bread, was not beloved by the ships' officers.) When the bombs struck, everybody in the wardroom was hurled to the floor amid a litter of chairs, tables, plates, silverware and fried bread. Shards of shattered glass fell on them and billows of smoke from ventilators and from the passageway swirled into the room. Some men jumped up and ran out, but several dozen others crowded in. For about half a minute—during which time flames were turning the hangar deck into an infernal cauldron—there were no explosions, and during this lull, O'Callahan had time to hurriedly offer up the words of a general absolution; there then began a series of huge blasts that rocked the carrier and presaged the horrors to come.

O'Callahan and the others in the wardroom scrambled for an exit. Several were already blocked, but one was clear of fire and smoke. They stumbled along a narrow, winding passageway as the smoke gradually overtook them, towards a forward ladder. As they passed parallel to the forwardmost of the carrier's three elevators, a gigantic blast demolished the elevator, ripped it off its track and sent it plunging into its well. O'Callahan's group, separated from the concussive pressure by only a bulkhead, shrank back, but fortunately, the thin steel panel held. They ascended past the hangar deck to the fo'c'sle, where the Padre paused at his office to don a helmet and pick up some vials of holy oil with which to administer the sacrament of Extreme Unction.

In the junior aviators' bunkroom, he found Methodist Chaplain Grimes Gatlin and some corpsmen tending a large number of badly wounded men. Gatlin and O'Callahan prayed with them, and tried very hard not to flinch at the ugly swishing sound that preceded (and announced) an imminent explosion. The overhead lights shortly went out, bathing the room in the dim, eerie phosphorescence of battle lights.

Gatlin whispered to O'Callahan, "Joe, I keep praying, Lord, I'm trying to keep these boys calm, don't let me show how frightened I am." O'Callahan understood perfectly.

All over the ship, men who were not actually wounded were palsied with shock. O'Callahan, leaving the bunkroom, passed several men in a passageway; one of them, glassy-eyed, trembled uncontrollably, and listened vacantly and with only the dimmest comprehension to the Padre's soothing words.

O'Callahan descended to a platform overlooking the hangar deck, which was by then nothing short of a blast furnace. In it, like fused ingots, the engines glowed a brilliant, demonic white that hurt the eye to look at. The heat drove O'Callahan back. He tried to make his way topside via the gallery deck, but flames barred his path. He retraced his steps to the fo'c'sle. There he daubed his face with anti-flashburn paste and donned long gloves, and made his way finally via some outboard catwalks to the flight deck, nine-tenths of which was immersed in flames. The remaining hundred feet or so was crowded with hooded fire fighters manning hoses, picking their way past clumps of men sprawled on the deck, some of them dead, some mangled, some unmanned by the holocaust.

Fire Marshal Stanley "Steamboat" Graham was exhorting, "Boys, we got pressure on the lines, we got hoses, let's get in there and save 'er." His enthusiasm seemed ill-placed.

Franklin was equipped with the latest in fire-fighting devices, into which considerable research had gone; as for example, fine-spray fog nozzles, far superior to solid spray nozzles. There were also 160-pound handy billies, 500-pound mobile pumps, and at every 100 feet of deck, a foamite system for generating flame-smothering foam. Most of these, however, were already unreachable. The carrier had 14 fire mains dependent on ship's power (which very shortly went out) and two operated by individual gas engines. In the face of the raging fire storm, these facilities proved hopelessly inadequate. At 8 A.M. destroyer *Miller* came alongside to train her hoses on the fire, but the puny streams also had little effect.

Miller took off Rear Admirals Ralph Davidson and Gerald Bogan and their staffs for transfer to *Hancock*. Just before leaving, Davidson advised Captain Gehres to abandon the ship, but the skipper, the final choice being his, elected to try and fight the raging of the flames. Gehres and the navigator, Lieutenant Commander Steve Jurika, remained on the bridge, which was completely cowled about with smoke and only intermittently visible. Gradually, the fire fighters rolled back the mantle of pall, recovering the deck almost as far aft as the island. *Franklin* was, by then, without power and dead in the water only 50 miles from Japan, an enticing target for Japanese bombers, especially since the gusting smoke was clearly visible many miles distant. Internal explosions continued to hurl large chunks of steel high in the air and to shake the carrier which, by 8:15, began to list to starboard. The island swung perilously out over the water.

O'Callahan leaned into the list and passed among the hurt and the fretful, administering last rites to the dying, comforting the wounded and cajoling the tremulous. He ignored a wound of his own—a piece of shrapnel had passed between his legs, slashing his left calf—until Doctor Sherman came over and saw to it. When the bombs first struck, Sherman had been hurled against the island and knocked out cold. Coming to moments later, the flight surgeon had immediately gone to work pulling mangled and senseless men away from the flames snaking up from the elevator pit.

There were several other doctors aboard the carrier. One, Doctor George Fox, had been in the ship's hospital ward with 11 patients and 7 corpsmen. The hospital was next to the chiefs quarters, where one of the bombs had struck, and was soon consumed by the searching flames. Another doctor, James Fuelling, was in the large mess hall amidships on the third deck, along with approximately 300 men, including Lieutenant Donald Gary, who was to win the other Medal of Honor. The mess hall was a death trap, with exit barred by flames in all directions and with a large cache of unexploded Tiny Tims stashed just forward. Fuelling helped stifle the tide of panic mounting in the trapped men by crisply ordering them to sit down on the deck and pray, which they did.

Gary, a Mustang up from the ranks, knew the ship very well. He thought he might be able to find an exit, and he had a rescue-breather which would help him survive the hot, searing smoke. He started off groping through the near-solid murk, falling over live bombs, shrinking away from bulkheads glowing with heat, and came finally to the fresh air spaces around one of the carrier's smokestacks leading up from the boilers. Gary squeezed in and slowly began scrabbling up the shaft, a very perilous venture. After he had climbed five decks in darkness, his hand scraped on a large jagged hole which an explosion had torn in the steel. He peered out and saw that he could drop from the hole to the safety of a gun platform. Gary took a few deep draughts of clean air, then started back down the pit.

O'Callahan, topside, continued to minister to the wounded, and had, by 9:30, tended everybody on the forward part of the flight deck, which was listing about 13 degrees to starboard. The cruiser *Santa Fe* came alongside and tried to rig lines for removal of the wounded, but was unable to hold her position. She snapped her lines and backed off, circling for another try. Cruiser *Pittsburgh* stood by to take the carrier under tow, if and when a messenger line could be winched across the water—a task complicated by the fact that *Franklin* no longer had power.

At the same time, radio messages came in to Gehres warning that radar screens had picked up a formation of enemy bombers which surely meant to try and finish off the crippled carrier. *Franklin* was in no condition to repel an attack. Most of her topside guns were either disabled or manned by corpses. Gehres' Marine orderly, Pfc Wally Klimkiewicz, requested permission to man one of the quad 40's forward. Gehres glowered at him and said, "What do you know about forty millimeters?" Affronted, the orderly drew himself up stiffly and said, "Sir, I'm a Marine." Klimkiewicz rounded up a crew consisting of mess stewards and headed for the gun.

The fires had, by then, been swept back abreast of the island, except for the forward elevator pit, from which gusts of flame and smoke continued to spurt. On the listing deck, large bombs rolled haphazardly, bowling men over as they went, and slamming against steel. Worst of all were the Tiny Tims, which sizzled and fishtailed erratically across the deck, knocking men senseless, in some cases ripping off limbs. When they exploded, the open flight deck turned into a slaughter house. The carrier's Executive Officer, Joe Taylor, called the scene "one of the most awful spectacles a human being has ever been privileged to see."

At 9:52, the worst explosion of the day occurred when the flames reached the after 5-inch ready-service magazine. The blast lifted the carrier out of the water. Men aboard her likened the experience to being shaken remorselessly by a giant dog. The flight deck was laid waste; men lay cringing as a noxious miasma engulfed them and a hailstone of steel began raining down, including airplane parts, entire engines, large sections of the ship itself and parts of human bodies. The men nearest the white center of the blaze flopped back like puppets in a windstorm, yet miraculously only two of them were wounded and none killed. When the pelting of steel ceased, O'Callahan and several others dragged the unconscious to safety. The fire fighters jumped up and went doggedly back to spraying the deck, and O'Callahan passed among a large number of men standing around, either too frightened or too confused to take part, and urged them to follow him back to the fires. The Padre was by then grimy with soot, his face a streaked mask of dirt, white globs of paste and driblets of sweat, and his only identification was his helmet, which had a white cross painted on it. After some coaxing, he managed to round up about eight or nine men and sent them to Lieutenant Lindsay "Red" Morgan, who was skidding and sliding along the deck, tilted by then 17 degrees to starboard, trying by himself to handle a hose under pressure.

As the flames which had originally devoured the hangar deck licked upwards, they raced unchecked through the gallery deck and, after touching off the after ready-magazine, began to threaten the forward one, where large numbers of 5-inch shells were stored. Lieutenant Commander William McKinney, the Gunnery Officer, commandeered several hose lines and struggled them towards the turret to drive back the flames. He and Marine Gunner Thomas Stoops and Ensign Robert Mc-

Crary began manhandling the shells over the side. O'Callahan, watching them, realized they couldn't possibly clear the magazine without help. He quickly gathered a small band of volunteers and led them into the turret, which was ringed by crackling flames and suffused with dark green smoke.

O'Callahan suffered from claustrophobia, which had hardly caused him more than minimal discomforts during his Navy career, but when he entered the turret, he suddenly found himself giving way to panic. Beads of perspiration stood out on his forehead; his breathing became labored. He steadied himself and with a great effort, bent to pick up a shell. Cradling it in his arms, he passed it along. The volunteers formed a fire brigade which snaked from the turret to the edge of the deck, where the last seaman flung the shells into the sea.

The heavy 5-inchers were hot enough to blister their fingers and bare forearms, and the men actually in the turrets quickly started coughing and gagging from the foul, acrid smoke. They lurched out, to be replaced by others. O'Callahan, out of a not entirely misguided sense of station, stayed until he thought he would pass out from the band of anxiety which threatened to cave in his chest, and then he relinquished his place in line and stumbled out into the fresh air. After a few minutes he force himself to go back inside. Until all the shells were jettisoned, he alternated periods of respite with periods of work. O'Callahan had rightly gauged the effect of his presence on the men. Many had begun to feel, with the innocence of men in extremity, that they were safe so long as they stayed close to the Padre. Inevitably, one of the men shouted, "Hey, look, the Padre's praising the Lord and he's passing the ammunition," a remark which fairly well represented their hope for survival; if they could simulate a good humor, destiny could hardly be cruel enough to overlook it. Ironically enough, those that followed the Padre were in the worst of the danger spots.

When the magazine had finally been cleared, O'Callahan felt his way out of the blistered turret and slumped wearily to the deck. His bones ached, his eyes stung, and he was bathed in a cold sweat. Gathering a strength he never knew he possessed, he roused himself and went off in search of more work to do.

Captain Gehres, observing this from the bridge, turned to Jurika and said, without further qualification, "O'Callahan is the bravest man I ever saw." Gehres was not a religious man, and was, on occasion, short of temper with chaplains who went among aviators preparing for a strike and "made them nervous." Subsequently, he was to admit to O'Callahan's mother that seeing the Padre's selfless bravery had given him pause. "If faith can do that for a man," he recalled thinking, "there must be something to it."

By 10:50, *Santa Fe* was back for her second try, and this time her skipper, Captain H.C. Fitz, decided to dispense with the amenities. Jurika, who was on the bridge throughout the disaster keeping a log, wrote, "She came alongside as though she were a well-handled gig making a liberty float at Long Beach." Fitz slid in at more than 22 knots, shearing off *Franklin*'s protruding gun ports, booms, and outboard catwalks, and ground to a halt flush against the carrier's dipping starboard side. "Greatest bit of seamanship I ever saw," Gehres gasped with admiration.

During the next hour and a half, some 800 men passed to the cruiser, some of them on foot but many in stretchers. In addition to the wounded, the air group personnel and other key (i.e., highly-trained) men not needed to fight fires also made the transfer, some of them unwillingly, and being very noisy about it. Among these was Sam Sherman, the Air Group surgeon, who flatly refused to go. "I'm a doctor," Sherman insisted. "Now the wounded are all off, but there may be more later." Gehres conceded the logic of this argument and gratefully overlooked the insubordination. Sherman stayed.

O'Callahan during this period continued to round up workers and direct them to Damage Control parties and to the ebullient "Steamboat" Graham. He also, because of his helmet, which made him readily identifiable, took to carrying out missions for Gehres as the captain called for them; at one point testing a gusher of water cascading over the side to make sure it wasn't gasoline, at another searching the ship for engineering officers who were needed on the bridge. When the captain ordered Graham to try and find rescue-breathers in Damage Control Station Eight—which was aft of the island and still engulfed in smoke—O'Callahan followed the Fire Marshal past one of the after 5-inch turrets still wreathed in flames. There the deck, which they could not see for all the smoke, had holes in it, through which they might easily have fallen into the fire pit below. It was slow, treacherous going, and the enclosure of smoke that blanketed everything from view threatened to make the Padre bolt with the dizzying panic that spiraled up in him, but as he later explained, "I didn't want to let Graham go alone." The Damage Control station was a gutted

211

shambles and so the trip had been for nothing, but rescue breathers were provided by *Santa Fe* just before she departed, and more important still, the cruiser used her winch to get a line from *Pittsburgh* to the stricken carrier for the towing operation, which was in the hands of Exec. Joe Taylor. At 12:25 *Santa Fe* cleared the carrier, and took up a station some 2,000 yards away, along with four or five circling destroyers, which were picking more of *Franklin's* crewmen out of the water; before dusk they had saved an additional 850 men.

The individual who personally saved the most lives that day was Lieutenant Gary, who had, upon finding a way to safety, returned through the black, tortuous windings of the pipes and ducts down five decks, crossed once again the compartment full of live bombs, and reached the mess hall where 300 men white with terror waited for the explosion that would wipe them out. The hatch to the compartment was dogged down, so Gary began banging on it with his flashlight, until it broke, then pounded with his fists. When the hatch opened, Gary stepped through and saw "a look of hope and anxiety on each man's face" which seared him. Gary hadn't, until then, fully appreciated how much of a burden had fallen on him. He led a group of the trapped men topside, then went down again. In all, he made the trip four times and was himself the last to leave. All 300 men were saved.

Elsewhere, others were trapped with less hope of rescue. In Steering Aft, five men were incarcerated in a dank, airless hole below a compartment which was completely flooded. The exit hatches had sprung their hinges and couldn't be opened. Gehres had promised Quartermaster Holbrook Davis, who fortunately had a functioning telephone line, that he would get them out, but he hadn't much of a notion how he could do this. O'Callahan came to the phone and asked Davis if they had battle lights. When Davis told him they did, he said, "Good, then play cards and pray until we get to you."

At just about that time, the squadron of enemy planes that had been tracked earlier in the morning arrived, and attempted to get through the combat air patrol to *Franklin*. Most of them were splashed, but one did break through and made a pass, which was deflected by Klimkiewicz and his crew of potato peelers. The bomber released too soon, and the bomb fell harmlessly 200 yards astern. At the quad 40's, the amateur gunners embraced each other joyfully and Klimkiewicz couldn't resist the temptation to glance smugly up at the bridge where Gehres was trying unsuccessfully to repress a huge grin.

O'Callahan left the bridge and came up to a group of men attempting to defuse a large bomb. When they told him to go away, he shrugged his shoulders and stood by airily while they finished the job, then walked alongside as they trundled it over the side.

A few moments later, he came upon "Steamboat" Graham, who was heading below to investigate whether hoses could be trained on the gallery deck from the hangar deck below it, which had, by then, been completely burned out. O'Callahan followed the young officer through a maze of passageways still clogged with smoke, so dark that even a flashlight couldn't penetrate the gloom. As they crawled along, they found themselves being scraped by the rims of crater-like holes in the deck, or passing over sodden, spongy shapes that might have been debris or dead bodies. For an awful moment,

213

O'Callahan experienced a nightmarish dislocation of perception—the flames, the smoke, the ugly, pervasive sense of death convinced him he was in Hell. The devil himself could have been hiding there, he shuddered, unfelt, unseen, unheard. He crept closer to Graham, who said squeamishly, "Don't push me, Padre."

About 20 feet along the passageway, they were able to peer into the hangar deck, which was by then relatively free of smoke. Sprinkled about like seedlings, random small fires burned dully and wisps of smoke curled and dissipated. It was hot, but not unbearable for short periods of time, Graham decided. He and O'Callahan went back up to the flight deck and led hose parties below.

During the next hour, O'Callahan stayed on the flight deck, manning a hose and periodically suggesting to one or another of his co-workers that they not aim the water directly at a bomb, an unfortunate habit which several had developed.

One man had carelessly played his stream directly at a warhead, spinning the arming vane, until hoarse voices brought him to his senses. "Look, kid," said one chief with unconscious humor, "let's not take any unnecessary chances."

As each foot of the deck was reclaimed from the smoke more live ordnance would appear, and the bombs would be steaming from the heat. Each in turn was washed down, defused by Lieutenant Commander George Stone and lugged to the edge of the flight deck to be cast overboard. O'Callahan, quite a bit older than most of the boys working the hoses, and utterly exhausted from the long hours under stress, nevertheless joined in. (He was much later, out of idle curiosity, to attempt it, and was

The *Franklin*, damaged, afire, and listing on March 19, 1945

able just barely to lift a 5-inch shell and not at all able
to carry it.) In his log, Jurika noted, "O'Callahan was everywhere, leading men, officiating at last rites, manning
hoses and doing the work of ten men."

At 2:35, while these operations were still in progress a
Japanese plane, fortunately not a bomber, managed
somehow to cross *Franklin's* deck with her wing guns
flickering. Lieutenant Commander Dave Berger, who
was fighting fires topside at the time, dove for cover, as
did everybody else who was exposed, except for O'Callahan, who was so engrossed in the job at hand that he
didn't even notice the spattering bullets reaming a stitch
in the deck. "There was Father O'Callahan," Berger recalled, "calmly walking along the flight deck carrying a
hose."

Shortly afterwards, the fire fighters had reclaimed

most of the flight deck, and with the discovery and subsequent dumping of a jumble of six 1,000-pound bombs,
the danger of further explosions finally ended, though in
every part of the ship small calibre ammunition continued to pop off and stencil the bulkheads, a great danger
to personnel, if not the ship. O'Callahan, for the first
time in twelve hours, allowed himself a moment of rest.
He sat down and relished the tiny breeze cooling his
parched skin. *Franklin*, taken under tow by *Pittsburgh*,
was making 6 knots, a ridiculous speed under normal
circumstances, but to the captain and crew, who for
many hours had thought they never again would see their
ship under way, it was a thrilling sensation. They wiped
the grime from their faces and grinned at each other
gleefully.

Throughout the remainder of the afternoon the carrier's engineers descended to the machinery spaces and
worked to restore steering, and to try to fire the boilers.
One of these teams, under Lieutenant Ed Wassman, finally managed to make good Gehres' promise to the men
trapped in Steering Aft, using hand pumps to clear the
flooded compartment above it. After 14 hours of playing
cards and praying (if that was, in fact, what they did)
Holbrook Davis and the other four men came topside
weak from their ordeal, and stared for long moments
with tears in their eyes at the stars just then coming out.

Many other rescue parties picked their way through
the fetid murk hoping to find survivors, but mostly they
found only burned, crushed and mutilated bodies.

At sunset, for the first time that day, provisions were
carted topside—bread and bacon fat for the officers,
bread and tinned sausages for the men—and wolfed

216

down as Navy food never has been and very likely never again will be. Exec. Joe Taylor, who was primarily responsible for the success of the towing operation, sighed happily, "Best damn meal I ever tasted."

During the night, the Japanese mounted an extensive foray in the hope of finishing *Franklin* off, but unaccountably, since she still had flames shooting up from her flight deck in the vicinity of the rear elevator, and was clearly visible in the darkness, the big battle took place some 20 miles distant, and the carrier was not molested. The following day, the engineers restored steering, *Pittsburgh's* towline was cast off, and *Franklin* rang up 12 knots unaided.

All that day, men worked tirelessly to render some semblance of order out of the chaos. There were searching parties which periodically found, in odd, inaccessible cubbyholes throughout the ship, wounded and unwounded survivors with blank, harrowed faces.

Other crews, with the assistance of four jeeps which were found undamaged in the forward elevator well, jettisoned vast quantities of rubble.

Other men worked to repair vital equipment, and certainly the most dolorous of all tasks, the recovery and burial of the dead, occupied more than 80 men working under the two chaplains. Throughout the day, the mournful refrain, "We now commit the bodies of our dead to the deep, and their souls to Almighty God," echoed again and again, incessantly, a sermon so subtle and sad it could have spoken for all the terrible years and all the mad agony of war except that it was itself doomed to die in the vast reaches of a very big ocean. The men who brought *Franklin* into Ulithi Harbor, 706

217

of them, formed a club which was known as the "706 Club," a fraternity of men who had passed very close to awful death, and who would do their best to forget it.

The war in the Pacific ended on August 14, 1945, with the Japanese acceptance of unconditional surrender. On September 2, the document was signed aboard the battleship *Missouri* in Tokyo Bay. Two days later, the island of Otori Shima was occupied by American troops, the Japanese flag lowered and the American flag raised. The name of the island was changed back to Wake.

Not all the volumes listed are of equal value or entirely accurate in all particulars, but all have supplied at least minor details to the narrative. In addition to the titles cited, I have had access to the facilities of the National Archives, the Marine Corps Historical Archives and the Navy Department Historical Archives. I am especially grateful to Captain Kent Loomis, U.S.N. (Ret.), Director of Naval History, for releasing to me certain documents previously classified and unavailable.

Personal communications from Rear Admiral, U.S.N. (Ret.) Rae Arison; Rear Admiral E.B. Fluckey, U.S.N.; Rear Admiral, U.S.N. (Ret.) Bruce McCandless; Colonel, U.S.M.C (Ret.) Mitchell Paige; Mr. A. Murray Preston; and Major General Frank C. Tharin, U.S.M.C., provided the major documentation for details in the narrative. Their courtesy and willingness to assist were unflagging, and are much appreciated.

I am also very much indebted to the following: Mr. Dean Allard, Navy Department, Historical Archives; Colonel F.C. Caldwell, U.S.M.C., Historical Branch; Lieutenant Commander D.M. Cooney, U.S. Navy Book and Magazine Branch; Lieutenant Commander Stanley Krohn, U.S. Naval Academy; and Mr. Frank S. Rodgers, National Archives.

Finally I cite my wife, Peggy, for service and good cheer far above and beyond the call of duty, or of marital vows, including the typing of a disorderly manuscript.

OFFICIAL AND SEMI-OFFICIAL DOCUMENTS AND PUBLICATIONS

Commander, Carrier Division 22, Narrative Report dated 10 October 1944.

Commander in Chief, U.S. Fleet, Battle Experience, Solomon Islands Actions, November, 1942.

Commander in Chief, Pacific, serial 00554, dated 18 February 1943.

Marine Fighter Squadron 211, Report of Operations December 4–20, 1941, dated 20 December 1941.

Marine Fighter Squadron 215, Action Reports, November, 1943 through February, 1944.

Marine Fighter Squadron 215, War Diary, November, 1943 through February, 1944.

Motor Torpedo Squadron 33, Action Report dated 17 September 1944.

Second Battalion, 7th Marines, Summary of Operations, 25–26 October 1942.

U.S.S. Barb, War Patrol Reports, numbers 8–12.

U.S.S. Franklin, War Diary, March, 1945.

U.S.S. Fulton, Rescue of Allied Prisoners of War, dated 30 September 1944.

U.S.S. Growler, War Patrol Report number 10.

U.S.S. Pampanito, War Patrol Report number 3.

U.S.S. Queenfish, War Patrol Report number 1.

U.S.S. Sangamon, Report number 32, AG-37, dated 16 September 1944.

U.S.S. Santee, Action Report dated 9 October 1944.

U.S.S. Sealion, Serial 08-44, dated 24 September 1944.

U.S.S. Sealion, Serial 09-44, dated 29 September 1944.

U.S.S. Sealion, War Patrol Report number 2.

U.S.S. Sigourney, Action Report, November 8, 1943.

Drury, Clifford M., *The History of the Chaplain Corps, U.S. Navy.* 5 Vols. Washington, U.S. Government Printing Office, 1948–1960.

Heinl, R.D., Jr., *The Defense of Wake.* (Marine Corps Monograph.) 1947.

Hough, Frank, *History of United States Marine Corps Operations in World War Two, Vol. 1.* Headquarters, U.S. Marine Corps, [1958–1963].

McMillan, George, *The Old Breed.* Washington Infantry Journal Press, 1949.

Miller, John, Jr., *Cartwheel: The Reduction of Rabaul.* Washington, Office of the Chief of Military History, 1959.

Rentz, John, *Bougainville and the Northern Solomons.* (Marine Corps Monograph.) 1948.

Roscoe, Theodore, *United States Destroyer Operations in World War II.* Annapolis, U.S. Naval Institute, 1953.

—— *United States Submarine Operations in World War II.* Annapolis, U.S. Naval Institute, 1949.

Sherrod, Robert, *History of Marine Corps Aviation in World War II.* Washington, Combat Forces Press, 1952.

Zimmerman, John L., *The Guadalcanal Campaign.* (Marine Corps Monograph.) 1949.

PUBLISHED WORKS

Bayler, Lt. Col. Walter, *Last Man Off Wake Island.* New York, Bobbs-Merrill, 1943.

Borroughs, John R., "The Siege of Wake Island," in Gene Z. Hanrahan, ed., *Assault!* New York, Berkeley, 1962, Chap. 1.

Boswell, Rolfe, *Medals For Marines.* New York, Thomas Y. Crowell Co., 1945.

Bowman, Marvin K., *Big Ben the Flattop; the Story of the U.S.S. Franklin.* Atlanta, Albert Love Enterprises, 1946.

Boyington, "Pappy," *Baa, Baa, Black Sheep.* New York, G.P. Putnam's Sons, 1958.

Bryan, J. III, *Aircraft Carrier.* New York, Ballantine, 1954.

Burns, Eugene, *Then There Was One. (The U.S.S. Enterprise and the First Year of War).* New York, Harcourt, Brace & Co., 1944.

Cunningham, W. Scott, With Sims Lydel, *Wake Island Command.* Boston, Little, Brown, 1961.

De Chant, John A., *Devilbirds.* New York, Harper & Brothers, 1947.

Devereux, James P.S., *The Story of Wake Island.* New York, Lippincott, 1947.

Dickinson, Lt. Clarence, *The Flying Guns.* New York, Charles Scribner's Sons, 1942.

Goette, John, *Japan Fights For Asia.* New York, Harcourt, Brace & Co., 1943.

Gurney, Gene. *Five Down and Glory.* New York, Ballantine, 1958.

Halsey, William, and Bryan, J. III, *Admiral Halsey's Story.* New York, McGraw-Hill, 1947.

Hara, Capt. Tameichi, *Japanese Destroyer Captain.* New York, Ballantine, 1961.

Hubler, Richard G., and De Chant A., *Flying Leathernecks*. Garden City, N.Y., Doubleday, Doran, 1944.

Leckie, Robert. *Strong Men Armed*. New York, Random House, 1962.

Lockwood Charles A., *Sink 'Em All; submarine warfare in the Pacific*. New York, Dutton, 1953.

Merillat, Herbert L., *The Island, a history of the First Marine Division on Guadalcanal, August 7–December 9, 1942*. New York, Houghton Mifflin, 1944.

Morison, Samuel Eliot, *History of United States Naval Operations in World War II*, Vol. III, *The Rising Sun in the Pacific*. Boston, Little, Brown, 1948.

——. Vol. V, *The Struggle for Guadalcanal*. 1949.

——. Vol VI, *Breaking the Bismarcks Barrier*. 1950.

——. Vol. XII, *Leyte*. 1958.

O'Callahan, Father Joseph T., *I Was Chaplain on the Franklin*. New York, MacMillan, 1956.

Okumiya, Masatake, and Horikoshi, Jiro, with Caidin, Martin, *Zero*, New York, E.P. Dutton, 1956.

Sakai, Saburo, with Caidin, Martin and Saito, Fred, *Samurai!* New York, E.P. Dutton, 1957.

Shirer, William L., *Berlin Diary*. New York, Alfred A. Knopf, 1941.

Sims, Edward H., *Greatest Fighter Missions*. New York, Harper & Row, 1962.

Toland, John, *But Not in Shame*. New York, Random House, 1961.

PERIODICALS

Baldwin, Hanson, "The Saga of Wake," *Virginia Quarterly Review*, Summer, 1942.

Karig, Walter and Manson, Frank A., "The Hairbreath Escape of the Barb," *Saturday Evening Post*, October 22, 1949.

McCandless, Bruce, "The San Francisco Story," *United States Naval Institute Proceedings*, November, 1958.

Reynolds, Quentin, "Chaplain Courageous," *Colliers*, June 23, 1945.

Sol, Martin, "Pick Us Up, Please!" *Argosy*, March, 1964.

Index

MacArthur, Gen. Douglas, 95, 125
Markuson, MoMM 1/C John, 182, 183, 186, 187
Maruyama, Lt. Gen. Masao, 49, 50
McAlister, Lt. John, 24, 25
McCandless, Lt. Cmdr. Bruce, 65, 71, 72, 74, 75, 78–81, 84–93
McCrary, Ens. Robert, 208, 209
McGuire, Maj. Thomas B., Jr., 104, 109
Medal of Honor, 63, 86, 96, 113, 149, 157, 174, 197, 206
Midway, 8, 32, 40, 41, 96, 172, 176, 192
Mitscher, Adm. Marc, 195, 196, 199
Morotai, 125, 128, 135, 144
Munda Field, 96, 110

Namkwan Harbor, 157, 162–164, 168, 172
Navy Cross, 19, 149, 174, 197
New Britain, 95, 114
New Guinea, 39, 41, 95, 109, 126
New Ireland, 110, 111, 112, 122
Newland, SC 1/C Lawrence, 183, 185
Nimitz, Adm. Chester, 32, 42, 125
Noumea, 65, 67

O'Callahan, Chaplain Joseph T., 195, 197–199, 202–204, 206–216
Oka, Col. Akinosuke, 49–51
Ondonga Field, 96, 109
Otori Shima, 37, 218
Owens, Maj. R. Gordon, 97, 104–106, 115–117, 123

Paige, Plat. Sgt. Mitchell, 39, 44–63
Pan American Airlines, 14, 15, 17
Peacock Point, 13, 14, 20, 23, 24
Peale Island, 10, 14, 15, 17, 25, 35
Pearl Harbor, 7, 8, 12, 13, 17, 20, 30–32, 35, 44, 72, 108, 126, 173, 176, 196, 198, 199
Pettyjohn, Cpl.. 54–56
Piva Village, 110, 118, 121, 122
Port Moresby, 39–41
Poulousky, Sgt. Tony, 24, 25, 27
Preston, Lt. A. Murray, 125–127, 132, 133, 135–144
Puller, Lt. Col. Lewis, 42–44, 49, 63
Putnam, Maj. Paul, 7–9, 13, 15–17, 24, 25, 27, 28, 33, 35–37

Rabaul, 48, 93, 95, 96, 98, 109, 110, 114, 118, 119, 123
Radio Tokyo, 23, 28, 29
Reich, Cmdr. E. T., 151, 153
Richard, MoMM 2/C James, 182, 186
Rogers, QM 3/C Floyd, 79, 85–88, 90
Roi Island, 28, 29
Roosevelt, Eleanor, 53, 54

Saint Andrews College, 197, 198
Sampler, Lt. Sam, 98, 101, 105, 123
Saunders, Chief Gunner's Mate Paul, 149, 167, 172, 183, 186–188
Savo Island, 66, 67, 69, 77, 79, 89, 93
Schonland, Lt. Cmdr. Herbert, 85–87
Scott, Rear Adm. Norman, 67, 68, 75
Seaman, Lt. Donald, 133, 135, 136, 138–143
Sever, SM 2/C Francis, 182, 185
Shank, Dr. Lawton, 18, 19
Sherman, Dr. Sam, 199, 205, 211
Solomon Islands, 39, 40, 95, 96, 98
Spears, Capt. Harold L., 117, 123
Sprague, Adm. Thomas L., 131, 132, 137
Stansberry, Cpl. Richard, 53–56
Stoddard, Lt. Eben, 133, 141–143
Stouffer, Lt. (j.g.) George, 138, 140–143
Summers, Cmdr. P. E., 151, 153

Tassafaronga, 66, 67
Tatro, Lt. Wilfred, 133, 141
Taylor, Cmdr. Joseph, 207, 212, 217
Teeters, Dan, 11, 13, 21, 30
Tharin, Capt. Frank, 11, 15, 18, 22, 24, 25, 26, 29, 30, 33, 35–37
Thompson, Ens. Harold, 128–131, 134, 137, 138, 140–145
Toki Point, 14, 25
Truk, 65, 67
Turner, Rear Adm. Richmond K., 67, 68

Uchida, Lt., 34–36
Ulithi, 199, 217
U.S. Naval Academy, Annapolis, 72, 149

Vandergrift, Maj. Gen. Alexander, 41, 43
Vella Lavella, 96, 105, 118

Wake Island, 7–11, 13, 19, 20, 22, 23, 25–27, 29, 31–33, 35–37, 39, 96, 173, 218
Walker, Lt. William, 177, 182, 185–191
Warner, Capt. Arthur, 98, 99, 101, 117
Wasile Bay, 127–129, 131, 132, 135, 142
Webb, Lt. Henry, 15, 16, 18
Wilbourne, Lt. Cmdr. William, 79, 80, 86, 89, 91
Wilkes Island, 10, 14, 21, 24, 35

Yale University, 11, 126
Yamamoto, Vice Adm. Isoroku, 65, 67
Young, Capt. Cassin, 70, 72, 78, 79, 81, 92